GROWTH THROUGH
MEDITATION
AND
JOURNAL WRITING

Growth Through Meditation and Journal Writing

A JUNGIAN PERSPECTIVE ON CHRISTIAN SPIRITUALITY

Maria L. Santa-Maria

Paulist Press New York/Ramsey

The Publisher gratefully acknowledges the use of "Psalm 139" from *Psalms/Now*, © 1973 by Concordia Publishing House. Used by permission.

Library of Congress
Catalog Card Number: 83-62471

ISBN: 0-8091-2570-6

Published by Paulist Press
545 Island Road, Ramsey, N.J. 07446

Printed and bound in the
United States of America

Contents

ACKNOWLEDGEMENTS

A work such as this one, which includes not only academic research, but years of personal and professional experience, is a journey which is never taken alone. I dedicate it to my parents who gave me life, love and support, when I most needed it, and to the friends and colleagues who persevered with me through the ups and downs of my personal and spiritual journey.

To Stephanie A. Deverick, M.D., a sustaining friend and colleague, who challenged me to make an explicit commitment of my faith, and who encouraged me to utilize my professional skills and gifts; to Judith S. MacNutt, M.A., whose love and acceptance gave me permission to cry and not have to be always strong; to Molly O. Alcott, Ph.D., therapist and friend, who walked with me into the dark corners of my emotional life and guided me into the light; to Sister Mary Ann Fatula, O.P., Ph.D., friend and spiritual guide, whose love and nurture helped to heal early wounds of my relationship to the church; to Sally and Ike Ross, Elders of Maximo Presbyterian Church, whose love and prayers have been like a special shelter of caring and protection; to Roy Clark, Ph.D., for his special friendship and editorial comments on this manuscript; to Roy Fairchild, Ph.D., of San Francisco Theological Seminary, who introduced me to Carl Jung and Ira Progoff, and who initially inspired this work; to Dr. Thomas A. Downs, advisor and friend, the most affirming human being I have ever met; and to the many participants of the Covenant Life Program, for their willingness to join me in this growth adventure.

Last, but certainly not least,
to my loving Lord,
who makes everything new,
and who transforms pain and suffering into
resurrection, joy and peace.
May this work bring those who undertake it
closer to him and render him much praise.

Foreword

As a psychotherapist in private practice, I have observed that many psychological problems of adulthood are symptomatic of a deeper spiritual concern, i.e., a search for life meaning and purpose and, ultimately, a search for God. The church is in constant search for creative learning alternatives regarding spiritual growth, which speak to contemporary human needs. I believe that the psychology of Carl G. Jung provides a unique perspective to deal with this problem, because it offers a bridge between the scientific and religious aspects of human experience.

Our Western society, with its focus upon technology and its excessive use of reason, has brought about an impoverishment of the spiritual life of individuals.

The thesis of this work is that Jung's concept of the feminine aspect of the personality, or the receptive mode, is essential in the development of a mature adult spirituality. This work reviews the universal search for meaning as a search for God (Chapter 1), the Jungian concept of the feminine or the receptive mode (Chapter 2), dimensions of Christian spirituality, as understood by Jungian writers (Chapter 3), and basic elements of classical spirituality and mysticism (Chapter 4). The last chapter consists of the development of an adult program of Christian spirituality (The Covenant Life) which includes seven dimensions: (1) Conversion—The Turning Point; (2) The Covenant in the Bible; (3) Prayer and Presence; (4) Mature Love and Relationships; (5) Reconciliation—Confession and Inner Healing; (6) Celebration and Community; (7) Ministry—The Fruit of the Holy Spirit.

The format of the program is a series of formal presentations on each of the above dimensions, followed by exercises in guided meditation and journal writing, entailing ten to fourteen hours. Guided meditation and journal writing were chosen as modes of expression because the former is a catalyst to contemplative prayer and the latter has been well established as a valuable instrument in secular programs, such as Ira Progoff's *Intensive Journal Workshop*. Each presentation consists of scriptural references and a short bibliography for each topic. It should be noted that whenever the words "he," "him," and "Father" are used to refer to God, the reader is reminded that God's Being is totally Other and surely not masculine in the human sense. When masculine pronouns are occasionally used for the deity in this work they are chosen advisedly, because of the current limitations of language.

The Covenant Life program has been proven to be an effective tool and context for psychological and spiritual growth. It is a modest attempt to develop a balanced approach to Christian spiritual formation. It clearly does not attempt to integrate all aspects of Jungian psychology into Christian spirituality. My hope is that research and writing on the feminine principle, as it pertains to adult spirituality in the Christian traditions, will develop even further in the years to come.

1

The Search for Meaning
Is a Search for God

The Problem

Most Americans allow themselves little time for listening to the inner self and for reflection on the meaning and purpose of human existence. The business of our existence coupled with this lack of reflection creates an imbalance which manifests itself, sooner or later, physically, psychologically, and/or spiritually. Those of us in the helping professions, such as counseling, ministry, social work or medicine, see the manifestations of this lack of centering in the problems and concerns that people share with us. Often, what is presented as a psychological or physical problem is symptomatic of a deeper concern. The discomfort points to a lack of meaning or purposefulness in life.

This phenomenon is not unique to those who seek counseling or medical assistance. Instead, this universal experience becomes manifest for each person at different stages of life. For many persons it becomes more explicit during the "middle years" (approximately after thirty-five). Usually, at this time there is a greater tendency for persons to turn to "inner" or more spiritual values, as opposed to external values such as material or objective achievements and accomplishments, (e.g., education, career, home, family). Carl G. Jung worked with thousands of persons in therapy during his lifetime and claimed that, without exception, those thirty-five or older expressed a deep concern regarding religious values and the ultimate meaning of life.[1]

For others, the urgency of the search for meaning in life is brought about by the death of someone near, or by a serious illness or another traumatic life experience. Elisabeth Kübler-Ross maintains that death provides a context for our lives; the terminally ill can experience a special sense of meaning which helps them to endure their suffering. Her own experience at a prison camp in Poland, after the war, enabled her to find her life goal. There, in the midst of suffering, poverty, and isolation, she decided to study medicine. She explains that the need for denial is evident, at first, among the terminally ill or where death is imminent, but later the individual can reconcile health with illness and mortality with immortality. Death and hope are permitted to exist side by side. But persons need the time and space to work through their suffering to achieve this stage of acceptance.[2] Death can be, then, an instrument which facilitates the human search for meaning because it reminds us to live life fully instead of merely passing through it.[3]

Those who lack meaning and purpose in their lives may also experience boredom. Viktor Frankl talks about the "Sunday neurosis" as the kind of depression which afflicts people who become aware of the lack of meaning in their lives when the rush of the busy week is over and the void within themselves becomes evident.[4] In addition, the individual human being has become less and less significant in our society in this era of big organizations, corporations and international and global concerns. This condition of lessened significance has produced an increased sense of apathy and a general lack of focused commitment to life and persons.

Karl Menninger addresses this concern in his book *Whatever Happened to Sin?* He claims that if there were a return to a sense of personal responsibility and accountability for ourselves and others, there would be an increased sense of life meaning and purpose among us all.[5]

One way in which the lack of meaning in life, brought about

by the middle years, death, illness, boredom, or the lessened significance of the individual in our society, is often manifested is in the search for a guru, i.e., the search for answers through techniques or persons outside of ourselves. Abraham Maslow, in his book *Farther Reaches of Human Nature*, talks about the experientially empty person who lacks directives from within and who turns to outer cues for guidance (e.g., clocks, rules, calendars, agenda and cues from other people).[6] The problem with this mode of coping is that no one can search for another. We each have to find our own meaning. What the guru knows that the seeker does not is that we are all pilgrims. Sheldon Kopp points out that before Siddhartha could discover that he needed no teacher, he first had to exhaust his longing for others to guide him and to take charge of his life.[7] Elizabeth O'Connor sums it up: "Having put the questions to ourselves, we need to trust the answers that come from within so that we are not demanding from others what must be discovered by tilling and tending the soil of our own lives."[8] It follows that the restlessness induced by the search for meaning can be redeemed if looked upon as an opportunity for personal and spiritual growth—a call or a challenge to be awakened from sleep, to take a new look at who we are and where we are going. We need to search not outward but inward. Confronting and discovering who we are becomes an essential part of the process.

To foster this kind of growth we must be aware of the conditions which nurture it. Anne Morrow Lindbergh, in *Gift from the Sea*, speaks of solitude as an important condition for personal and spiritual growth.[9] Discovering our inner selves requires time and space for reflection and quiet. The stumbling block for most of us is that we need to relearn to be alone, for most of us fear it. This relearning will entail a shift in the way we live.

We fear solitude because we associate it with loneliness, whereas physical distance between persons has little or nothing to do with loneliness. It is psychological distance that makes the difference. Robert Pirsig, in *Zen and the Art of Motorcycle Maintenance*, explains that technology is often blamed for fostering loneliness, because loneliness is associated with new technological devices such as TV's, jets, freeways, etc. But the real problem is not the objects of technology, but the tendency of technology to isolate people into impersonal attitudes of objectivity. It is the dualistic way (objective vs. subjective) of looking at things underlying technology that produces the depersonalizing effects.[10]

Obstacles to the Discovery of Meaning

A brief historical overview will help here. Up to the eighteenth century, the inner life was traditionally referred to as the area of the soul. In the nineteenth century, philosophers wanted to reclaim the last domain of "superstition" from the church. They wished to make the inner life subject to the laws of causality, an area free of mystery, and therefore the concept of the soul was abandoned for the concept of the self. The development of the latter was extensively studied from the time of childhood onward. As a result, symbolic, abstract and spiritual phenomena such as language, thought, morality, etc., could be studied as socio-psychological products and not as divine interventions. The problem that emerged with this orientation is that human beings were thereby deprived of a sense of mystery which is essential to human nature and to the search for ultimate meaning and purpose.[11]

One of the giants of humanistic psychology, Abraham Maslow, attempts to resolve the dichotomy and claims that in human peak experiences, which are accessible to us all, these polarities (objective vs. subjective) are transcended or resolved. Consequently, there is a movement toward unity and integration of the world and reality.[12] He claims that the dichotomy has been one of the problems of organized religions, i.e., a tendency to polarize the mystical and individual vs. the legalistic and organizational. Although there is always some tension between these, the religiously mature person should be able to integrate these two trends to a great extent. It is not uncommon to observe that many persons forget the subjective religious experience (such as knowing a personal God and/or the conversion experience) and redefine religion as a set of objective or external habits, behaviors and dogmas which become empty and in the truest sense anti-religious.[13]

The functions of the right and left brain hemispheres (which are fairly recent discoveries in human physiology and psychology) become relevant at this point. Each of us has two major modes of consciousness, one linear and rational and the other non-rational and intuitive. These two functions correspond to the two brain hemispheres. The left hemisphere, connected to the right side of the body, controls analytical and logical thinking (especially verbal and math functions). Its mode of operation is primarily linear and it processes information sequentially. The right hemisphere, connected to the left side of the body, specializes in holistic mental functions. It is primarily responsible for a person's orientation to space, artistic endeavors, crafts, body image and recognition of faces. It processes information more diffusely than the left hemisphere and is more relational than the latter.[14]

Our Western educational systems largely concentrate on the verbal and intellectual functions. We lack a learning system for the functions associated with the other side of the brain. Therefore, the approaches which are useful in the search and discovery of the inner self will be foreign to most of us, at first. It can be said, however, that more and more persons are moving into disciplines such as meditation, neglected in the West for a long time, which aim at personal rather than intellectual knowledge, and which are designed to produce a shift from the active, outward-oriented, linear mode toward a receptive and quiescent mode.

Where Meaning Is Found—
Some Promising Directions

Having discussed some of the functions, approaches and environments which help or hinder the search for the inner self, we must look at the overall context in which meaning-making takes place. Speaking of the Christian experience Sam Keen believes that if one is to discover the holy it must be in one's own biography, not in the history of Israel.[15] To conclude that we should discard the message of God's covenant with Israel is to miss the point of his statement. What Keen is saying is that we must look at the context of our personal life story, i.e., relate our very own life experience to the God of the covenant, who did intervene in the pilgrimage of the Israelites.

If we are to find meaning at all we must be willing to look at ourselves, at our lives, and must therefore be willing to take time to be alone. The desire not to be alone is an unwillingness to be with oneself; one is like a person lost in the wilderness. John Dunne, in *Time and Myth*, tells of three basic movements in the human life story. The first is a movement of crisis, of dividedness (such as death, illness, boredom, estrangement, etc.); the second is a movement of withdrawal, or aloneness; and the third is a movement of return, of all-oneness, of wholeness. In order to arrive at the heights one must be willing to make the journey from one extreme to the other.[16] Solitude and withdrawal provide the opportunity for encountering one's inner self and for return to wholeness. Therefore, the essence of the human life story is one of conversion and of movement, of transformation from one level of awareness and integration to another, where there is a breakdown but also reintegration, and one's sense of reality is thereby significantly altered.

Maslow refers to mature and whole persons as self-actualizing people. These persons generally possess the following characteristics: (a) they are involved in a cause outside of themselves, and have overcome the work vs. joy dichotomy; (b) they are reconciled with evil and suffering, in the sense that they understand its occasional inevitability and necessity in the context of life meaning; (c) they are apt to be profoundly more religious or spiritual; and (d) they are more integrated regarding the relationship between inner values and outer life involvements.[17] I prefer to understand these as tendencies where the polarities do remain to some extent. The presence of the polarities becomes, then, the source of a creative tension which helps us to grow and motivates us to continue our search for wholeness.

However, the search for ultimate meaning goes beyond self-actualization, because human existence is essentially self-transcendent. Frankl claims that we need to stop asking about the meaning of life and instead think of ourselves as those who are being questioned by life (God) daily.[18] Paul Tournier, the Swiss

Christian psychiatrist, maintains that the search for meaning is ultimately a search for God, because it is the supreme and universal need of humans to find God.[19] In other words, the search for ultimate meaning is a religious search, a search for God, and thereby a question of faith, in which a person moves through his or her own personal existence searching for meaning in each life event or experience.

The search for meaning and the faith experience itself are non-rational. They are not arrived at through a series of logical syllogisms. The basic nature of our experience of God is intuitive, subjective and personal. The reasoned argument is hindsight, in our effort to articulate our experience in a way that is intelligible to others. Jung's definition of the "feminine" aspect of the personality becomes relevant here, as a *modality* of being which focuses on the non-rational, the intuitive and the personal. This concept will be elaborated upon in Chapter 2.

Simone Weil speaks of the search for God as an ongoing hunger for proving that God exists:

> Here below we must be content to be eternally hungry; indeed we must welcome hunger for it is the sole proof we have of the reality of God, who is the only sustenance that can satisfy us. The danger is not lest the soul should doubt whether there is any bread (God), but lest, by a lie, it should persuade itself that it is not hungry.[20]

Carl Jung saw the traces of the divine imprinted on the most hidden layers of the psyche, as its origin, and as the symbol of wholeness toward which it strives.[21] This can be a psychological way of saying that we were created in God's image (Gen 1:26–27). We, therefore, surrender to the will of God when we surrender to the deepest nature of our humanity. This surrender itself brings about an internal freedom which enables us to take the risk to search within ourselves.[22]

> We need the engagement with self to find out that we have our houses resting on sand, but there is no possibility of getting them over on rock without an engagement with God.[23]

The journey to the deepest part of ourselves, i.e., the ultimate search for meaning involves three aspects: an engagement with oneself, an engagement with God, and an engagement with others. Only by engaging in all three movements can one correct the imbalance of a life lacking meaning and purpose.[24]

For the Christian, his/her life story in the context of the Scriptures, along with prayer, worship and the sacraments, and mature relationships with others, is the primary means for the engagement with God. But, ultimately, the kind of engagement that needs to take place is subjective and personal. Walter Wink points out, in *The Bible in Human Transformation*, that traditional biblical criticism failed to penetrate the object of the Scriptures and be in communion with it. Scholars failed in not being in communion with their inner selves, and in not allowing the biblical text to penetrate through their own persons into this part of their being. If we want to engage with God through the Scriptures, we must ask ourselves how the text resonates within us, because what the text evokes depends upon our own personal life experience. If we approach the Scriptures in this manner, the understanding of ourselves which the text evokes will make possible a more profound understanding of what the text actually says.[25] In the same manner, it can be said that in many of our Christian churches the worship experience and the sacraments have lost their symbolic power and have become, instead, empty rituals. We must rediscover the personal religious experience that these represent, in order that they may become for us, once again, a source of spiritual nourishment. In the end they will bring us closer to our center, in which we find that communion with God is our ultimate purpose for being and without which there is no hope for wholeness of fulfillment.

The purpose of this chapter has been to look at our human condition in light of the need for a conscious commitment to spiritual growth, a personal spirituality. Life experiences such as reaching the middle years, the death of someone close, illness, boredom, and the lessened significance of the individual in our society are among the conditions that precipitate a search for meaning which is written into the fabric of our being. Through the search inward—in solitude, looking at the personal and subjective within us, encountering our own life story in light of the Scriptures and rediscovering the power of religious symbols—we find that God is the ultimate object of our search. It is essential, therefore, to develop a way of living (a spirituality) which will nurture, support and guide our search for the spirit within us.

The remaining chapters of this work will explore the following: Jungian approaches to the inner life and the feminine aspect of the personality and how these can serve as catalysts for Christian spiritual development (Chapter 2); an overview of several contemporary and classical approaches to spirituality which emphasize non-rational functions (Chapters 3 and 4); a suggested contemporary model for adult spirituality to be utilized by individuals and/or groups (Chapter 5).

Notes

1. Calvin S. Hall and Vernon J. Nordby, *A Primer of Jungian Psychology* (New York: Mentor Books, 1973), p. 92.

2. Elisabeth Kübler-Ross, *Death and Dying* (New York: Macmillan, 1969), p. 41.

3. *Idem, Death, the Final Stage of Growth* (Englewood Cliffs: Prentice-Hall, 1975), p. 123.

4. Viktor E. Frankl, *Man's Search for Meaning* (New York: Simon and Schuster, 1959), pp. 108–109.

5. Karl Menninger, *Whatever Happened to Sin?* (New York: Hawthorne Press, 1973), p. 188.

6. Abraham H. Maslow, *Farther Reaches of Human Nature* (New York: Viking Press, 1971), p. 33.

7. Sheldon B. Kopp, *If You Meet the Buddha on the Road, Kill Him!* (New York: Bantam Books, 1972), p. 62.

8. Elizabeth O'Connor, *Journey Inward, Journey Outward* (New York: Harper & Row, 1968), p. 14.

9. Anne Morrow Lindbergh, *Gift from the Sea* (New York: Pantheon Books, 1955), p. 42.

10. Robert M. Pirsig, *Zen and the Art of Motorcycle Maintenance* (New York: Bantam Books, 1974), p. 350.

11. Ernest Becker, *The Denial of Death* (New York: Macmillan, 1973), p. 191.

12. Abraham H. Maslow, "Religion and Peak Experiences," *Psyche and Spirit*, ed. John J. Heaney (New York: Paulist Press, 1973), p. 103.

13. *Idem, Religions, Values, and Peak Experiences* (New York: Viking Press, 1970), pp. vii–viii.

14. Robert E. Ornstein, *The Psychology of Consciousness* (New York: Penguin Books, 1972), p. 67.

15. Sam Keen, *To a Dancing God* (New York: Doubleday, 1973), p. 104.

16. John S. Dunne, *Time and Myth* (New York: Doubleday, 1973), p. 104.

17. Abraham H. Maslow, *The Farther Reaches of Human Nature*, p. 291.

18. Viktor E. Frankl, *Man's Search for Meaning*, p. 77.

19. Paul Tournier, *The Meaning of Persons* (New York: Harper & Row, 1957), p. 32.

20. Simone Weil, *Waiting for God* (New York: Harper & Row, 1951), p. 35.

21. Regina Bechtle, "C. G. Jung and Religion," *Psyche and Spirit*, ed. John L. Heaney, p. 76.

22. Elizabeth O'Connor, *Journey Inward, Journey Outward*, p. 35.

23. *Ibid.*, p. 21.

24. *Ibid.*, p. 10.

25. Walter Wink, *The Bible in Human Transformation* (Philadelphia: Fortress Press, 1973), p. 33.

2

The Inner Life
and the Feminine Mode

The Human Life Stages

The purpose of this chapter is to provide an understanding of the feminine modality in the context of the inner life and a personal spirituality. In order to appreciate Jung's understanding of the inner life and the feminine, I want to give a brief overview of the human life stages and their significance regarding spiritual growth.

Psychologists have studied extensively the periods of infancy, childhood, adolescence and the aging process, but until the last ten or fifteen years, adult development (approximately from the twenties to the fifties) has not received much attention. Recently, a number of popular books have been published on the subject. Carl Jung and Erik Erikson initiated the concept of the middle years and the stages of adult development. For our purposes here, I will focus primarily on the thoughts of Jung and Jungians.

Jung outlines the human life stages, roughly, as follows: (1) childhood, extending from birth to puberty; (2) youth, extending from puberty to middle life (approximately thirty-five to forty); (3) adulthood, extending approximately from the middle years to the late fifties; and (4) old age, extending roughly from the sixties until death. Developmental tasks are attributed to each period, although a person's chronological age may or may not coincide with his/her level of psychological development.[1]

During the first half of life, i.e., the first two stages, the person generally concentrates upon his/her own individual development in relation to the outer world. For example, most of the concerns are geared to one's emotional and financial independence, career, family and outside achievements. Whereas, during the second half of a lifetime, beginning in the third stage, the individual tries to recenter his/her life around spiritual values and a search for ultimate life meaning. Jung speaks of these two lifetime periods as the "morning" and the "afternoon" of life. He comments that persons are often unprepared for the tasks of the latter and, therefore, develop what we know as a neurotic condition, because they cannot "live the afternoon of life according to the program of life's morning."[2] The search for spiritual values and the meaning of life, typical of life's "afternoon," is an inward search. Let us consider what Jung and Jungians have to say about the subject.

The Inner Search

Many middle-aged persons, having been successful in their chosen career, suddenly awake to a feeling of emptiness and a lack of meaning in their lives. Edward Edinger, in *Ego and Archetype*, says that the question "What is the meaning of life?" is actually unanswerable. Instead, we must ask "What is the meaning of my life?" This question leads us to the task of discovering our own personal identity, and the adequate answer can only come from within.[3] Jung asserts: "I early arrived at the insight that when no answer comes from within to the problems . . . of life, they ultimately mean very little. Outward circumstances are no substitute for inner experience."[4]

Dr. James Hillman, a Jungian analyst, points out the importance of the inner search in the context of human relationships. He believes that in order to relate significantly to another, one must be in touch with his/her inner self. If one attempts to relate

otherwise, the relationship is likely to become one of dependency, where persons lose their identities and hinder one's development.[5] Such an outcome turns out to be self-defeating, because personal development runs parallel to the discovery of meaning.

Jung regards the development of personality as "fidelity to the law of one's own being." He refers to the New Testament word "pistis" which means "fidelity" in Greek. He claims that it has been erroneously translated as "faith" and that it means trust, a trustful loyalty. He believes that the overall goal of human development (individuation in Jungian terms) lies in fulfilling one's own destiny and vocation.[6] Similarly, Ira Progoff, in *Jung, Synchronicity and Human Destiny*, comments that an implicit purpose is contained in each organism (human or not) and that purpose may or may not be actualized. It may either develop in a stunted form or not develop at all. But it is from this purpose within that we derive the meaning of our personal lives.[7]

Along the same line of thought, Frances Wickes, in *The Inner World of Choice*, affirms that human beings realize themselves through the individual choice of vocation.[8] This is consistent with Jung's thinking: he claims that the choice of vocation distinguishes a person as a unique human being, individual and separate from others. Here vocation means more than a given job or occupation. It suggests a lifestyle, in other words, one's overall purpose and approach to life. For Jung, "vocation acts like a law of God from which there is no escape. . . . Anyone with a vocation hears the voice of the inner man: he is called."[9] The choice of vocation is not forced upon us. We consciously say yes or no to it. The conscious choice is essential to the fulfillment of our unique personalities.[10] I believe that the concept of vocation indicated here includes a spirituality, because it involves a choice of personal values, and it defines one's overall and ultimate purpose and relationship to God, others and the world.

To summarize so far, the inward process by which we discover the meaning of our lives begins with a question of personal identity, a confrontation with ourselves. Such a confrontation enables us to discover our inner purpose, and to relate to others in a wholesome and mature manner. This profound self-discovery manifests itself in the unique choice of vocation. Vocation encompasses a spirituality, i.e., a choice of values, a lifestyle; it defines our basic approach to life, including God, others and the world.

Neurosis and the Absence of Meaning

In his autobiographic work, *Memories, Dreams and Reflections*, Jung shares his conviction that meaninglessness inhibits the fullness of life, and it is, therefore, equivalent to illness. With Frankl (see Chapter 1), he affirms that meaning makes many things endurable—perhaps everything.[11] About one-third of the persons that Jung saw in therapy were not suffering from any clinically definable neurosis. Their problem stemmed primarily from the lack of meaning and purpose in their lives.[12] In his clinical experience, Jung also saw individuals become neurotic when they contented themselves with inadequate or mistaken answers to the questions of life. Some persons seek position, marriage, reputation, outward success or financial security, and remain unhappy and neurotic, even after they attain what they were seeking. In Jung's view these individuals are usually confined within too narrow a spiritual horizon. They need to broaden their concepts of life and its meaning.[13] Jung makes a significant contribution to the understanding of personality because he insists that neurosis should not be regarded as something entirely negative. It can point to a new possibility of development for the individual, a new starting point.[14] I agree with Jung, and I find this viewpoint particularly helpful in the context of counseling. If clients are helped to see that concern which motivates them to seek counseling as a new starting point, their energy level is evoked and the whole counseling process itself becomes one which is redemptive indeed. We have discussed the search for identity and meaning; in the next section, we see how these relate to religious experience.

The Inner Search and Religious Experience

In order to develop a philosophy of life that is true to who we are, we must learn to distinguish between what has been drummed into us and what we have acquired by our own experience and knowledge.[15] Although the Bible says "The kingdom of God is within you" (Lk 17:21), most people seek it only outside of themselves. In *The Undiscovered Self,* Jung states that the basis of faith is not rationality but spontaneous religious experience, which brings the individual's faith into immediate relationship with God. He believes that the unconscious is the source of our religious experience.[16] Unfortunately, by emphasizing doctrines and customs of the church, many of the Christian denominations have thrown into the background the question of personal religious experience.

Religion is one of the earliest and most universal activities of the human heart and mind. Jung believes that it is an instinctive attitude peculiar to humans and that its many manifestations can be followed throughout history.[17] For most persons life can go on smoothly without religion for a period of time, but when suffering comes, people begin to reflect about the meaning of life and its bewildering and painful experiences. About his patients in the second half of life, Jung says that none of them was really healed who did not regain his/her religious outlook.[18] "The decisive question for man is: Is he related to something infinite or not? That is the telling question of his life."[19] For Jung, the individual who is not anchored in God can offer no resistance, on his/her own resources, to the difficulties normally encountered in a lifetime.[20]

In response to those who claim that religious experience cannot be validated in a scientific way, Jung says that no matter what the world thinks about religious experience, the one who has it possesses a great treasure. Such an experience provides a person with a source of meaning that gives him/her a new awareness and perspective about the world. In Jung's words: "He has 'pistis' and peace. . . .Is there any better truth about ultimate things than the one that helps you to live?"[21]

From Jung's perspective, God is a primordial experience which is characteristic of being human, and from the earliest times humanity has tried to express this experience, to assimilate it or else to deny it.[22] Jung believes that there is no such thing as chance or accident. On the contrary, he experiences ordinary happenings as meaningful. He views chance as a symptom of an alienated life, of one not in touch with his/her inner self. For the person of faith, as for the child and the primitive, says Jung, chance does not exist.[23] Instead, life's events are part of a meaningful plan or design, with a definite purpose. In my opinion, this kind of faith statement, coming from one of psychology's giants, cannot be simply overlooked. Once again Jung builds a bridge between psychology and religion in dealing with the question of the meaning and purpose of life.

The Emergence of a Religious Life

The significance of religious experiences is that they can convert one, i.e., they literally turn one around to the point of recognizing one's intimate relationship with a source of meaning beyond oneself. For Jung, every neurosis is basically an expression of a disturbance of the religious function of the psyche, which he regards as its fundamental function. If it is inhibited or blocked, humans tend to fashion substitute gods for themselves and thus impoverish their inner life.[24]

> As often as he (man) put another content in his center in place of God—whether it were a beloved partner, money, nation or any other "ism"—and made it a surrogate for God, he becomes its victim to his own destruction.[25]

When a person relates to his/her religious instinct consciously, it works toward a wholeness of the personality. When this instinct is ignored, repressed or displaced, this frustrated religious instinct produces despair, depression and illness, just as much as would repression of any other vital human instinct, such as sex or aggression.[26]

In the development of a relationship with God, it is important to distinguish between God and the image of God that is being experienced by the individual as a psychological event within his/her being. In other words, we should not confine God, exclusively, to our own personal experience.[27] The experience is a psychological event because it takes place within the human psyche.

But the psyche is only the place; the event itself transcends the psychological, because it draws the person beyond himself or herself into a relationship with God.[28] Another way of saying this is that God is more than our image and experience of God.

For Jung, another important concern has been that many Christians have failed to relate their inner selves to their external belief systems. The encounter with Christ has been viewed as an experience from without instead of from within the inner self.[29] If, as we encounter Christ within, we dared to interpret his teachings in a personal and subjective manner, we would find powerful insights about human development which are relevant for our own age. In Edinger's words: "Seen in this light, Jesus' teachings become a manual for promoting individuation."[30]

Ann and Barry Ulanov, in their book *Religion and the Unconscious*, outline three stages of ego development which also relate to the emergence of a religious life and a relationship to God. The first is a pre-ego stage in which the ego is identified with and undifferentiated from the unconscious, much like the identification of an infant with the mother. In the second stage, the ego establishes his/her own domain with regard to the unconscious and the external world. For example, the individual begins to define who he/she is and what he/she can or cannot do. In the third stage, the ego adopts a value beyond itself (a transpersonal value in life), one which goes beyond personal concerns. This occurs without diminishing the person's own individuality.[31] In other words, there is a movement from dependency to autonomy, where the needs for dependency continue to be nurtured to some extent and a new sense of autonomy emerges. The Ulanovs point out that love provides the necessary space between self and others for this kind of interdependent growth to occur.[32]

> ps offer the best example of the way an ego is
> o move outside of itself, whether in the process of
> ve and moving into a sustained intimacy with an-
> n, or in the course of having a child . . . or in the
> of a spiritual relation to God.[33]

..chors describe the need of the ego to become disidentified with (or separated from) the unconscious, in the second stage, as that state of becoming spiritually poor in the Gospel Beatitudes. Another way of saying this may be a person's willingness to stand alone without the security of family or a given group. More will be said about this in the next chapter. The Ulanovs see this ability to become poor as a requirement for the encounter with that which is beyond the self—i.e., God. In becoming poor we empty ourselves; we let go, we surrender. The willingness to become poor is essential to the development of a religious or spiritual life.[34] The capacity for containing and accepting our emptiness (our poverty) draws upon and necessitates a development of the feminine aspects of the personality, both on the part of women and within the personalities of men.[35] For the feminine aspect of the personality is the home of solitude and receptivity. And these make a mature relationship with God and other persons possible. More will be said about solitude in the next chapter.

Briefly, then, in ego development, as in the development of a relationship with God, love (which is also a function of the feminine) enables us to move from an undifferentiated and unconscious state (from a lack of awareness of our identity and our relationship with God) to a stage of clarification, of personal identity (of meaning, purpose and relationship). Through the experience of separateness, of aloneness, of spiritual poverty, we come to a new sense of values, a new sense of life—vocation which takes us beyond ourselves into a relationship with God and the world.

This concept of psychological and spiritual birth and rebirth is not new. For thousands of years rites of initiation have been teaching rebirth of the spirit. Jung says that "every individual needs revolution, inner division . . . and renewal."[36] Edinger, along the same lines, believes that aloneness and alienation are a prelude to rebirth and religious experience.[37] Such rebirth is the question of Nicodemus in Scripture: "How can a man be born when he is old? Can he enter a second time into his mother's womb and be born?" (Jn 3:4). For the Christian, the conscious choice of a personal relationship with Christ is the beginning of a new life, both psychological and spiritual.

The Significance of the Symbolic

As it has been suggested earlier in this chapter, humans are incapable of expressing God, because as soon as we speak of God we use the traditional images of our language. Consequently, human talk about God is generally symbolic or mythological. The basis of Jung's statement about religion is that God cannot be completely captured by any human words or description.[38] Therefore, the religious function, i.e., the drive to relate to a transpersonal source of meaning (God), often manifests itself in the production of images and symbols. It is precisely the world of symbols which establishes a link between the psyche and religious experience.

The excessive use of reason (the latter pertains to the masculine function), which is prevalent in our culture, reinforces reliance on the outer forms of religion. It creates a duality between the head and the heart. The symbol, on the other hand, unifies the rational and the non-rational and the conscious and the unconscious; because the image speaks to the whole person—mind, heart, senses, experience and imagination—it engages one more fully than does a mental or rational concept.[39]

Jung believed that religious symbols give meaning to human life. He claimed that the existence of human beings will never be satisfactorily explained without a sense of living mystery which can be expressed only by symbol.[40] Dr. Hillman speaks of the importance of cultivating one's inner world of images, because it is essential for what he calls the religious moment. The religious moment requires a receptive mood to God's intentions for us. The visions of our personal futures come to us first in dreams, images and fantasies. This receptivity through which we receive the revelation of God's intentions for our lives is feminine in nature.[41] Furthermore, Jung indicates that the impoverishment of the interior life of contemporary Christians and the decreasing vitality of Christian symbolism result in large part from a loss of connection with the feminine mode of being. The recovery of the feminine element will bring about the rebirth of vital religious symbolism within individuals, churches and in society in general.[42]

The symbolic mode has a relational and mediating function. Emphasizing the importance of symbols and meaningful ritual, Jung speaks of human ritual as a means of responding to the actions of God upon us. In other words, symbols and ritual activate us spiritually and enable us to render back something to God in a manner deeper than words or reason.[43] Language is essential for clarity of thought, but the most profound truths can only be expressed indirectly in images, symbols, poetry, music and color.[44] The feminine mode of being, postulated by Jung as an archetype (a psychological construct common to all persons), can be understood only through images, emotional responses and behaviors.

The Feminine as a Modality of Being

History shows that women and feminine values have been painfully oppressed in our society for a very long time. Even at the present time in the United States there are serious discrepancies between the employment opportunities and benefits given to men vs. women. In Freudian psychoanalytic literature, women are often dealt with as inadequate males, and they are treated almost exclusively from the point of view of masculine psychology. Within the structure of the Christian (and Jewish) church denominations there are many instances, even today, of prejudice, discrimination and oppression of women and feminine values in areas of government, liturgy, ordination to the pastorate and spirituality. The tendency has been to treat sexual differences as inferiorities of women in relation to men.

In Genesis we read: "God created man in his own image; in the image of God he created him; male and female he created them." "Man" refers to humankind as a species, from the word *âdâm* in Hebrew. This word is to be differentiated from the other Hebrew meanings of the word "man," which may imply sex or gender, such as the words *iysh* and *zâkâr* meaning man as an individual or a male person, respectively. God's image is to be found in the complementarity of male and female. Ulanov says that the first concrete manifestation of the covenant between God and his creatures is to be found in the relationship of man and woman.[45] The many analogies in the Old Testament regarding God's relationship with Israel as a marriage (see Hosea, Jeremiah, Song of Solomon and Isaiah), as well as many New Testament references (e.g., Jn 1:18; 12:23; Mt 5:5; Gal 3:28), suggest the importance of feminine values and the equality and complementarity of men and women in the sight of God. This clearly shows that prejudice toward the feminine modality is not consistent with the Christian biblical perspective. My view is that where the Bible appears sexist, it is a function of semantics, culture and the human limitations of the writer and not God's intent overall.

Although we cannot look to Jung exclusively for a precise definition of the feminine, he did make a significant contribution to psychology by initiating a new approach to the feminine. Jung saw the feminine as a category of being with its own unique values and strengths. Ann Ulanov, in her excellent work *The Feminine*, discusses the three traditional approaches to the feminine as biological, cultural and symbolic. The biological approach, prevalent in the Judaeo-Christian tradition, is primarily that of Freud: "anatomy is destiny." Here the psychology of the feminine derives from what the female body lacks—a phallus. In the context of this approach the psyche is not recognized as an autonomous element in itself. The cultural approach is proposed by the neo-Freudian Karen Horney and the well-known anthropologist Margaret Mead. From the point of view of this approach, the psychology of the feminine derives primarily from the influence of cultural tradition; custom and habits mold the psychological propensities of women, as well as society's definition of the feminine. It follows that feminine traits may be changed if our culture changes. The third approach she calls the symbolic, promoted primarily by Jung and Jungians. Here the nature of the feminine is not confined only to females; instead, personal wholeness is achieved by an awareness of contrasexuality, i.e., the discovery and development of the masculine and feminine in each of us.[46]

Regarding the biological approach we can say that it has been demonstrated that woman has recessive male characteristics—male sex hormones in the bloodstream and in rudimentary male sex organs—and that man has, likewise, recessive female characteristics. But although maleness and femaleness are genetically determined, they occur as a result of a relative predominance of one set of characteristics vs. the other. The point here is that gender determination is not absolute but relative, and that masculine and feminine elements exist in a complementary relationship to each other.[47]

Jung broke new ground when he separated concepts of sex and gender and was able to see the masculine apart from maleness and the feminine apart from femaleness. He called the masculine in woman "animus" and the feminine in man "anima." Intrinsic to Jung's thinking is the notion that wholeness of the individual depends on understanding both masculine and feminine elements. Not only our own individual growth, but our relationships with others are severely hampered by a lack of understanding of either one of these elements.[48] We, therefore, must think of ourselves no longer as exclusively masculine or feminine but rather as whole beings in whom the opposite qualities are also present. Consideration of the masculine-feminine polarity is very important because, for Jung, the whole psyche is structured in polarities, and it is the tension generated by these polarities which provides the primary energy of life.[49] Unfortunately, it is not realistic to attempt to discuss fully in this work Jung's proposed structure of the psyche. Consequently, the following discussion will be limited to characteristics of the feminine modality of being and its role in the development of a spirituality.

Characteristics of the Feminine

Dr. June Singer, a Jungian analyst, maintains that if we truly allow ourselves to be who we are, we discover that we are all androgynous. However, being true to ourselves may not be this simple, since most of us have been conditioned to underestimate feminine values in our culture. It may take many of us quite some time to unlearn certain habits and thought patterns which undervalue the feminine, and to develop new ones which will allow the feminine to emerge.[50] The feminine and its psychology describe not only factors that contribute to sexual identity, but certain modalities of being such as styles of awareness, ways of relating, ways of internalizing reality, and modes of making judgments and decisions about it. These modalities express themselves in images, behavior patterns, and emotional respons-es.[51]

Jung talked about the anima (feminine) and the animus (masculine) in terms of "Eros" and "Logos" respectively. He used these terms as conceptual aids, in order to show that feminine consciousness is more characterized by the connective quality of Eros than by the discriminating and cognitive quality associated with Logos.[52] Anima (Eros) is the function of relatedness, diffu-sive intuition and awareness. This diffuse awareness is the place where children live until we educate them out of it.

In diffusive awareness and intuition a content presents itself whole and complete. For Jung, it is a kind of instinctive apprehen-sion; it is a non-rational function of perception. Its contents have the character of being given, in contrast to the derived or pro-duced character of analytical thinking.[53] By the use of the term "non-rational" Jung does not mean that the feminine is contrary to reason but, instead, it is something which is beyond reason, i.e., not grounded on reason.[54]

Knowing in the context of the feminine, never loses its vital connection with loving, i.e., it always remains in the context of relationship.[55] This knowing is an inner knowing; thought comes later as an after-thought which scrutinizes the action or event and assesses its value.[56] Irene C. de Castillejo, in her book *Knowing Woman*, says that the basic masculine attitude toward life, with-in both men and women, is that of focus, division and change. The feminine (in either sex) is more nearly an attitude of accep-tance, an awareness of the unity of all life and a readiness for rela-tionship.[57]

The feminine within a man gives relationship and related-ness to his consciousness, just as the masculine within a woman gives to her consciousness a capacity for analytical reflection, de-liberation and self-knowledge.[58] In other words, the anima is a personification of all feminine psychological tendencies in a man's psyche, such as prophetic hunches, receptiveness to the non-rational, capacity for personal love, feeling for nature and his relation to the unconscious.[59] It is erroneous to stereotype wom-en as "emotional and irrational" and men as "logical and ratio-

DIAGRAM #1

TWO MODES OF CONSCIOUSNESS

RECEPTIVE (FEMININE)	ACTIVE (MASCULINE)
Right brain	Left brain
Primary experiences	Secondary experiences
intuition	sensation
creativity	logic
feeling	thinking
simultaneous	sequential
diffused	focused
unitive	divisive
accepting	discriminating
wisdom	knowledge
insight	proclamation
unconscious	conscious
perception	judgment
personal	cognitive
artistic	technical
imaginative	verbal

nal." Rather, men and women have both masculine and feminine attributes which are more or less predominant, depending upon the uniqueness of their physical, psychological and cultural makeup and environment.

In an address given at a Jungian conference in San Francisco, Dr. Katherine Brodway commented that women who are able to communicate inner awareness tend to identify two parts of themselves, each part having both positive and negative aspects. One part is experienced as the "feeling" (appreciative or reflective) side or for many their feminine side. It is the part that cares for people and for all life, the part that can enjoy the non-competitive creation of things, the part that needs some time for space and solitude, for just being. In its negative aspect, it is the part that sometimes feels dependent. But there is also another side ("the masculine") that relishes meeting a competitive challenge and craves honors, recognition and achievements, the part that wants to "slay a dragon or two," win contests and make a difference, not just in the context of the family, but in a national and global context, as well as in history. In its negative aspect, this part can get in the way of relating because in wanting to be first it pushes others aside or manipulates them.[60] (See Diagram #1 for examples of the two modes of consciousness.)

The expression of the feminine can be elementary and static or transformative and dynamic. Each of these two aspects can be expressed in a positive or negative manner, as indicated in the above paragraph, depending upon whether growth and development are promoted or hindered in the individual. We experience these various aspects of the feminine through images, emotional responses and behaviors. Appendices A and B, at the end of this work, provide an overview of categories of the feminine principle and examples of these. (For an even fuller description, see Dr. Ulanov's book, *The Feminine*, pp. 157–162.)

Spirituality and the Feminine

Jung believed that women are naturally more receptive than men to the spirit of God through their femininity. He also maintained that it is through the feminine aspect of his personality that the male mystic relates to God, because the feminine's relation to nature and to God is more familiar and intimate than that of the masculine.[61]

Within an individual, there are four kinds of development or stages of awareness of the feminine aspect of the personality: The first stage is primarily conceived as merely instinctual and biological in nature; the second stage is that in which the perception of the feminine is romantic and aesthetic in character, but it is still influenced by sexual elements; the third stage raises love to include a spiritual aspect of relationship; and the fourth stage is self-transcendent and characterized by a responsive wisdom about life and relationships. According to the Jungian analyst Dr. Marie L. VonFranz, this last stage of maturity regarding the feminine is rarely reached by persons in our day and age.[62]

James Hillman maintains that maturity in love requires the

development of the feminine within us, because the feminine is that which gives birth and nourishes us to believe in God and in ourselves. It helps us to be open to ourselves just as we are.

> I do not know how better or how else we can prepare for the religious moment than by cultivating, giving inner culture to, our own unconscious femininity.[63]

Prayer and meditation are particularly akin to the feminine. One important aspect of prayer, which leads to contemplation, has been described as an active silence in which one listens and becomes receptive to God, letting it happen rather than trying to make it happen. This receptive attitude is akin to the feminine modality.[64]

There is no such thing as spirituality in a vacuum. Spirituality implies relationship and receptivity in its very essence. Therefore, spirituality is, by its very nature, related to the feminine.

For the person who has developed both his/her masculine and feminine modalities, there is no dichotomy between spirit and body because it is in the body that the spirit dwells. Similarly, religion is not different from ordinary life, but rather it is an intensification and deepening of it. The feminine seeks to create unity from duality.

Ulanov believes that for the feminine the experience of God is always individual and personal. In other words, it is in a particular moment, to a particular person, that a particular event occurs, and a spiritual transformation occurs in a particular person's heart. We grow in the knowledge of God through very concrete and personal experiences in our lives. God touches us in specific ways, times and places. The feminine is the means which enables us to touch God and have God touch us. A transformation takes place as we seek to find God in the hidden meaning of the concrete happenings of our lives.[65]

> For the feminine spirit there is an indissoluble bond between sensual and religious passion. . . . True feminine wisdom is from the heart, as well as from the head; it seeks the holy in

the lowly, finding where it can be the sanctifying power of the Holy Spirit.[66]

Jesus' means of communication through parable, symbol and living example is expressive of the feminine modality of consciousness and spirit. Loss of the feminine means loss of all those aspects of life associated with it, loss of fullness of interiority, loss of a true and wholistic sense of the human personality, and, therefore, of a full spiritual life.[67]

The activity of the feminine is to accept a conception, to carry knowledge, to assimilate it, and to allow it to ripen. It is a mixture of attentiveness and contemplation. This readiness to receive and respond with one's whole being is essential for religious experience and spiritual growth.[68] Emma Jung writes that the art of prophecy[69] can be ascribed to the feminine because receptivity is a feminine attitude. If we neglect the feminine we block our capacity for psychological and religious vision. The feminine mode of activity is to attend to things, to keep still until the insight has come. The feminine encompasses the intrinsic modes of religious meditation because its sense of time is always of the moment. Time is qualitative rather than quantitative; it is "kairos" rather than "chronos."[70]

To sum up, we can say that the feminine makes us more receptive to the spirit of God and that it enables us to love others more completely, or in a more integrated fashion. It allows us to see God in our concrete life experiences and thus to be transformed. Ultimately, it is the means to prayer, contemplation, and a personal spirituality.

In this chapter, I have attempted to give an overview of the significance, characteristics and symbolic manifestations of the inner life and the feminine mode of being. I have discussed how the feminine becomes relevant: (1) initially, during the middle years with the search for life meaning and purpose, and (2) later, as the inner search for identity and vocation lead the person to religious experience, the encounter with God, and the development of a personal spirituality. In the next chapter, several contemporary approaches to spirituality will be reviewed and evaluated from this perspective.

Notes

1. Carl G. Jung, "The Stages of Life," *The Portable Jung,* ed. Joseph Campbell (New York: Viking Press, 1971), p. 17.

2. *Idem, Modern Man in Search of a Soul* (New York: Harcourt, Brace, & World, Inc., 1933), p. 108.

3. Edward F. Edinger, *Ego and Archetype* (Baltimore: Penguin Books, 1973), p. 108.

4. Carl G. Jung, *Memories, Dreams, Reflections* (New York: Vintage Books, 1965), p. 5.

5. James Hillman, *Insearch: Psychology and Religion* (New York: Charles Scribner's Sons, 1967), p. 37.

6. Carl G. Jung, *Collected Works,* trans. R.F.C. Hull, Vol. 17: *The Development of Personality* (New York: Princeton University Press for the Ballinger Foundation, 1954), p. 63.

7. Ira Progoff, *Jung, Synchronicity, and Human Destiny* (New York: Dell Publishing Co., 1973), p. 63.

8. Frances G. Wickes, *The Inner World of Choice* (Englewood Cliffs: Prentice-Hall, 1963), p. 281.

9. Carl G. Jung, *Memories, Dreams, Reflections,* p. 340.

10. Ann Ulanov and Barry Ulanov, *Religion and the Unconscious* (Philadelphia: Westminster Press, 1975), p. 20.

11. Carl G. Jung, *Memories, Dreams, Reflections,* p. 340.

12. *Idem, Modern Man in Search of a Soul,* p. 61.

13. *Idem, Memories, Dreams, Reflections,* p. 140.

14. *Idem, Two Essays on Analytical Psychology,* C.W. Vol. 7, p. 46.

15. Jolande Jacobi, *The Way of Individuation,* trans. R.F.C. Hull (New York: Harcourt, Brace & World, 1965), pp. 128–129.

16. Carl G. Jung, *The Undiscovered Self,* trans. R.F.C. Hull (Boston: Little, Brown and Co., 1957), p. 100.

17. *Ibid.,* pp. 36–37.

18. *Idem, Modern Man in Search of a Soul,* p. 229.

19. *Idem, Memories, Dreams, Reflections* p. 325.

20. *Idem, The Undiscovered Self,* p. 34.

21. *Idem, Psychology and Religion* (New Haven: Yale University Press, 1938), p. 114.

22. Jolande Jacobi, *The Way of Individuation,* p. 52.

23. Edward F. Edinger, *Ego and Archetype*, p. 101.

24. Ann Ulanov and Barry Ulanov, *Religion and the Unconscious*, p. 53.

25. Jolande Jacobi, *The Way of Individuation*, p. 106.

26. *Ibid.*, p. 55.

27. Ann Ulanov and Barry Ulanov, *Religion and the Unconscious*, p. 53.

28. Ira Progoff, *Jung, Synchronicity and Human Destiny*, p. 84.

29. Frieda Fordham, *An Introduction to Jung's Psychology* (Baltimore: Penguin Books, 1953), pp. 74–75.

30. Edward F. Edinger, *Ego and Archetype*, p . 136.

31. Ann Ulanov and Barry Ulanov, *Religion and the Unconscious*, p. 176.

32. *Ibid.*, p. 181.

33. *Ibid.*, p. 182.

34. *Ibid.*, pp. 188–189.

35. *Ibid.*, p. 273.

36. Carl G. Jung, *Two Essays in Analytical Psychology*, p. 5.

37. Edward F. Edinger, *Ego and Archetype*, p. 52.

38. Aniela Jaffè, *The Myth of Meaning*, trans. R.F.C. Hull (New York: Penguin Books, 1975), p. 103.

39. Ann Belford Ulanov, *The Feminine* (Evanston: Northwestern University Press, 1971), p. 95.

40. Carl G. Jung, *Man and His Symbols* (New York: Dell, 1964), p. 215.

41. James Hillman, *Insearch: Psychology and Religion*, p. 108.

42. Ann Belford Ulanov, *The Feminine*, pp. 109–111.

43. Carl G. Jung, *Memories, Dreams, Reflections*, p. 253.

44. Irene Claremont de Castillejo, *Knowing Woman* (New York: Harper & Row, 1973), p. 142.

45. Ann Belford Ulanov, *The Feminine*, p. 293.

46. *Ibid.*, pp. 140–141.

47. *Ibid.*, pp. 163–164.

48. *Ibid.*, pp. ix–x.

49. *Ibid.*, p. 13.

50. June Singer, *Androgeny* (New York: Doubleday, 1976), p. 276.

51. Ann Belford Ulanov, *The Feminine*, p. 142.

52. Carl G. Jung, *Aion*, C.W. Vol. 9ii, p. 14.

53. Carl G. Jung, *Psychological Types*, C.W. Vol. 6, p. 453.

54. *Ibid.*, p. 454.

55. Frances G. Wickes, *The Inner World of Choice*, p. 228.

56. *Ibid.*, pp. 204–205.

57. Irene Claremont de Castillejo, *Knowing Woman*, p. 15.

58. Carl G. Jung, *Aion*, p. 16.

59. *Idem, Man and His Symbols*, p. 186.

60. Ute Dieckmann, Katherine Brodway and Gareth Hill, *Male and Female, Feminine and Masculine* (San Francisco: C.G. Jung Institute, 1973), p. 10.

61. June Singer, *Androgeny*, p. 307.

62. Carl G. Jung, *Man and His Symbols*, p. 195.

63. James Hillman, *Insearch: Psychology and Religion*, p. 126.

64. *Ibid.*, pp. 21–22.

65. Ann Belford Ulanov, *The Feminine*, pp. 183–189.

66. *Ibid.*, p. 304.

67. *Ibid.*, p. 134.

68. *Ibid.*, pp. 172–173.

69. Emma Jung *Animus and Anima*, trans. C.F. Baynes and H. Nagel (New York: Spring Publications, 1957), p. 55.

70. Ann Belford Ulanov, *The Feminine*, pp. 175–177.

3

Elements of Contemporary Christian Spirituality

Having established that God is the ultimate Object of the search for meaning and wholeness (Chapter 1), and that the feminine, as a modality of being, is an essential factor in the spiritual growth journey (Chapter 2), we now turn to more practical considerations of what we refer to as Christian spirituality.

Spirituality Resists Definition

While researching this subject, I have become increasingly aware of the lack of understanding among the majority of Christians regarding the term "spirituality." Much to my surprise, it is a very vague and confusing term for most Christians (with Catholics and perhaps some Anglicans being the only exceptions). I believe that the lack of clarity is due to the fact that spirituality, like the feminine modality, resists definition. It is like the Beethoven sonata in the story that Henri Nouwen tells in his *Genessee Diary:*

> When Beethoven had played a new sonata for a friend, the friend asked him after the last note, "What does it mean?" Beethoven returned to the piano, played the whole sonata again and said, "That's what it means!"[1]

Christian spirituality is a way of life, a lifelong and transformative process, for adults only. It is the protective umbrella out of which the kingdom of God is born and established within each individual. It is much like Dr. Elizabeth Howes' definition of the feminine: she calls it the "vessel which, impregnated, gives birth to the divine child or self which is in each of us."[2]

It involves the realization of the human personality, according to the inner plan established within each one of us by God. This does not mean that it is the kind of phenomenon for which ten easy steps can be indicated; for spirituality is simple and yet complex. Guidelines for its development do exist, but there are also obstacles and dangers which must be considered regarding these. Many books have been written about it, while at the same time, it cannot be taught exclusively in an abstract or theoretical fashion.

Much unlike the definitions of spirituality in *Webster's Dictionary*, mature Christian spirituality must become incarnate, or take flesh, in each one of us. Just as the Son of God became incarnate in Jesus of Nazareth, Christian spirituality manifests itself as a supportive discipline which makes possible the growth and practice of our faith in a mature and balanced fashion. Without a developed spirituality our faith is superficial and meaningless, possibly even pathological.

Spirituality is the Christian's approach to the wholeness that God intends for each person, individually and as a community. It is the living-out of the Spirit of Jesus within us. Its key elements include: (1) a deep knowing of the person of Jesus and through him of the Father and the Holy Spirit; (2) a mature understanding of the human personality; (3) the disciplined practice of prayer; (4) the experience of mature love; (5) an awareness of the nature and reality of evil; (6) an appreciation of the meaning of celebration in the context of Christian community; (7) sharing the goodness of God's life and love with others in order to further the kingdom. The purpose of this chapter is to develop basic elements of Christian spirituality, which are addressed by contemporary Jungian theologians.

Conscious Choice—Rebirth

The beginning of the Christian spiritual journey requires a conscious choice and commitment, a decisive turning point. Unless there is such a conscious choice and commitment there is no ensuing journey. Howes and Moon, in *Man the Choicemaker,* say that "the distresses of choice are our chance to be blessed."[3] In the beginning of Matthew's Gospel we find the figure of John the Baptist personifying the need for a change of heart (metanoia), a turning around, in the familiar theme of repentance. This kind of self-confrontation is essential in order to enter the inner way of the kingdom.[4]

John Sanford, an Episcopal priest and Jungian analyst, says that this conscious choice must be an individual act. It cannot be accomplished through a group identification.[5] This is crucial because even among Christians there are many who fall into the misconception that a person can be simply reared into the faith, i.e., that a conscious and decisive point is not necessary for salvation or wholeness in the Christian sense (the word "save" in the Synoptic Gospels means to heal or to make whole). Such consciousness is also a prerequisite for psychological maturity and moving into what we call the stage of adulthood (see Chapter 2).

Because in making such a conscious choice and commitment an individual differentiates himself or herself from the group, a certain degree of anxiety can be expected as one accepts responsibility for that choice. The aloneness at that moment cannot be avoided. It is a moment of crisis, the Greek word for which means separation or turning point. A peculiar characteristic of this choice is that "we can never . . . return to the condition in which we were before our crisis, without the scope of our personality being reduced."[6] In psychological terms we call this return to the previous condition "regression." Likewise, it is conceivable to speak of a spiritual regression.

What is the nature of the conscious choice or commitment of which we speak? It has to do with taking a stand regarding our ultimate life values, i.e., declaring a commitment to what we believe about life and the world and living our lives accordingly. This is the crux of psychological and spiritual maturity.

The ultimate focus, for the Christian, relates to the identity of Jesus of Nazareth, in the context of his view of life and the world. In the Gospel, Jesus asks Peter: "Who do you say that I am?" (Mt 16:16; Lk 9:30). The individual's personal answer to this question marks the beginning of his/her entry into the fullness of the kingdom. From this point on, the encounter and relationship with the person of Jesus becomes an integral part of the person's everyday life, the starting point for his/her spiritual transformation and/or rebirth. Meditation on the Scriptures is probably the most direct and powerful means of growing in the knowledge of the person of Jesus. More will be said about the Scriptures and practical approaches to meditation later in this work.

Creative Solitude—The Womb

Solitude is the womb of Christian spirituality, the space which nourishes, which allows for the birth of the new creation or the newly transformed self. Nouwen believes that most of us have lost contact with the source of our own existence and have become "strangers in our own house . . . we avoid confrontation with our deepest selves" and therefore we avoid solitude.[7] Both he and Kelsey advise us to unhook from the activity which is so typical of modern living,[8] so that we can make time and space for solitude in our lives.

To live a spiritual life we must first find the courage to enter into the desert of our loneliness and to change it by gentle and persistent efforts into a garden of solitude. This is a difficult task because, as Nouwen says, it is hard for us to believe that the dry and desolate desert can yield a variety of flowers.[9] But it is precisely silence and solitude which free us from ordinary perceptions and attitudes and offer us a creative and fresh outlook of life and reality. As stated in Chapter 1, the movement from loneliness to creative solitude requires, to some extent, a withdrawal from the distractions of the world, though we must remember that the solitude that counts is a solitude of the heart, an inner quality, i.e., an attitude that does not necessarily depend upon physical isolation.

It is important, in the development of a mature spirituality, to keep a careful balance between silence and words, withdrawal and involvement, distance and closeness, solitude and community.[10] Kelsey points out that every devotional master, from Jesus to Thomas Merton, suggests times of quiet for the development of spirituality. This is the basic meaning of the commandment to keep the sabbath a holy day.[11]

We know that there are some key experiences which come to us when we are with other people and some which come to us only when we are alone. The Christian life does not take away our loneliness, but it protects and cherishes it as a precious gift. When we are able to create a lonely place in the middle of our actions and concerns, our successes and failures slowly can lose some of their power over us.[12] Consequently we are freer to be true to ourselves and we see that silence can be an experience of death and resurrection. It is a temporary cessation of one's doing and planning and desires. The difference in the purpose of silence and detachment between the East and the West is that in the West detachment is for the purpose of achieving a richer attachment with God and with other human beings,[13] whereas in the East the goal is to lose the self completely. We see that the secret of Jesus' ministry is hidden in that lonely place where he went to pray, early in the morning, long before dawn (Mt 1:32–39). It is in this lonely place, where Jesus enters into intimacy with the Father, that his ministry is born.[14]

> Is God present or is He Absent? . . . In the center of our sadness for His absence we can find the first signs of his presence. In the middle of our longings we discover the footprints of the one who has created them.[15]

The Gift of Prayer—The Child

If solitude is the womb, then the gift of prayer is the child of Christian spirituality, or the fruit of the reborn self. It is the way in which the deepest part of us touches God and we are touched by him. It is difficult to talk about it because it cannot be encapsulated or boxed in. Its nature is somewhat paradoxical and, like a person's love life, it is a most intimate aspect of one's life. For these reasons it is frequently described in an oversimplified manner. Generally, what is closest to our person is most difficult to express and explain.

In a sense prayer is a universal instinct. All human beings have found themselves, at one time or another, praying automatically, without having to think about it.[16] Yet, the paradox of prayer is that we have to learn how to pray, while we can only receive it as a gift. Prayer is a gift from God. We cannot truly pray by ourselves. It is God's Spirit that prays in us. This gift is within our reach because, in Jesus of Nazareth, God has entered into our lives in the most intimate way, so that we could enter into his life through the Spirit (Jn 16:7).[17]

Henri Nouwen uses an insightful analogy in describing the experience of prayer. He says that we are like asthmatic people who are cured of their anxiety, because the Spirit has taken away our narrowness (the Latin word for anxiety is "angustia" which means narrowness), and made everything new for us. Consequently, the new life—new breath—which we receive is the life and breath of God. Prayer is God's breathing in us.[18] It is not simply coincidence that most contemplatives train themselves to be still and readied for prayer by focusing upon the rhythm of their breathing. When we become depressed in our spiritual life, we have forgotten that prayer is a gift; that is precisely the meaning of grace.[19] The thing to do, then, is not to try to pray harder, but, simply to ask the Spirit to do it for us (Rom 8:26–27).

Since prayer is a gift-grace, its timing cannot be easily manipulated by us. All we can do is nurture certain conditions and foster the kind of activities which will make us ready to receive the gift. Waiting patiently in expectation is the foundation of the spiritual life and prayer. [20] This waiting is not of a passive nature. It is a period of learning, because the longer we wait, the more we learn about him for whom we are waiting.[21] In the journal written by Nouwen at the Genessee monastery, he comments:

> God's grace is like a gentle morning dew and a soft rain that gives new life to barren soil. Images of gentleness. My call is indeed to become more and more sensitive to the morning dew and to open my soul to the rain, so that my innermost self can bring forth the Savior.[22]

The primary problem for most Christians in developing a prayer life is to make it top priority. Most of us have a very difficult time figuring out how to develop a mature prayer life, when our lives are so busy with work, family, friends, etc. If we do set aside some time, we usually end up wondering about all the other things that we still have to do. It always seems that there is something more urgent and more important than prayer. Nouwen says that the only solution is a prayer schedule that you will never break without consulting your spiritual director. More will be said about the latter later in this work. He advises us to set a time that is reasonable and, once it is set, to stick to it at all costs.[23] But often we set aside time at the end of the day for prayer when we are too tired to do anything else. The result is that nothing happens and then we wonder why. It is important that we set aside for prayer the time when we are most alert, most aware and most conscious.

Most Christians would tend to define prayer as conversation with God. In practice this means, for many, relating to God a list of requests about our needs and wants and the needs and wants of others who are important to us. Usually this tends to become a one-way conversation, at best. This is only one aspect of prayer. It is called intercessory prayer. For the mature Christian, who seeks to develop a personal spirituality, prayer does not stop here. He/she seeks to grow into a deeper experience of prayer, which writers on spirituality refer to as contemplation or contemplative prayer. The word contemplate comes from the Latin and it means "to behold," to "gaze intently or attentively" at something or someone. In contemplative prayer we focus our attention completely upon the person of God and his presence within us. It is something that we experience, as opposed to something that we do. This is very difficult for most of us in the West. We are accustomed to being very performance and activity oriented. When we try to experience prayer in this fashion, for a while it may seem that nothing happens. But if we stay with it and look back over a longer period of prayer, we realize that something has happened. What is most close, most intimate and most present to us, often cannot be experienced directly but only with a certain distance.[24]

When we talk about making time and space for God and

prayer in our lives, it does not mean that we must exclude all our ideas and attachments from our awareness while we pray. We can include these in our prayer, directing our attention primarily to God and bringing each concern that we have into his loving presence. Nouwen suggests that in this way we can experience a new perspective and liberation in regard to each of our concerns.[25] Consequently, when we are serious about prayer, we no longer consider it one of the many things people do in their lives but, rather, a receptive attitude out of which all of life can receive a new vitality.

Just as artists, writers and therapists search for the style that is most uniquely theirs in what they do, people who pray sooner or later will ask themselves the question: "What is my way to pray?" "What is the unique prayer of my heart?"[26] Each person will have an individual way of relating the totality of his/her being to God. One needs to know oneself and the strengths one has been given, so that they can be used in seeking and responding to God and developing a personal spirituality.[27]

We must remember also that prayer is not void of pain and suffering. But, as Nouwen says, the pain is so deep that you do not want to miss it, since it is in this pain that the joy of God's presence can be tasted. This seems close to nonsense but, as Nouwen continues, "it is beyond sense."[28] When we choose to enter into prayer, regardless of pain, we enter into the intimacy of God where all human suffering is embraced and transformed by a divine compassion.[29] Therefore, we can say that contemplation is the beginning of the union with God that is to be fulfilled in the resurrection, at the end of time; it is a taste of what is to come.[30]

In this section we have discussed some issues about the nature of prayer. Practical suggestions about developing a prayer life will be elaborated later in this work.

Love and Relationships

The key word for a mature spirituality is balance. While a certain degree of introversion is essential for developing a spiritual life, we cannot afford to forget that God is so deeply interested in the physical world that he became incarnate in it. He is so deeply concerned about real human beings that Jesus became a man and he lived and died and rose for us, and he wants us to become friends and sharers of his kingdom with him.[31]

True love and compassion belong to the center of Christian spirituality and the contemplative life.[32] Compassion means to enter into the suffering of another with passion, to love him or her deeply and intensely. It does not mean loving at a distance, or loving when it is comfortable, or loving when it does not hurt. It means getting in there, jumping in with both feet, even if it means getting dirty and bruised. Either Jesus of Nazareth was the Son of God, who lived on this earth, suffered, died and rose for us or he was not and did not. There is no in-between. There is no such thing as a Christian on the fence. If we are on the fence, we are not Christians. Our Christian commitment, our prayer life and our actions cannot be separated, for they are of the same fabric.

Kelsey, in *The Other Side of Silence,* says that Christian meditation and the inner way are like a spiral staircase. The first steps bring us to a realization of the nature of the God to whom we are giving ourselves. Then if we are serious, this requires that we put into action what we have learned, coming to a new level of caring for others. Once we are trying to act upon the meaning which we have found, we are ready again for a new level of prayer or meditation; then again with new insights into the reality of the risen Christ, we are given another new understanding of what our actions ought to be, at an even deeper level, and a new basis for directing them and so on. In other words, as each level of experience is actualized in our relationships, we find again and again new levels of awareness and inner communion with God. This process is infinite, and it is the only way for mature Christian social action and relationships, i.e., those which grow from our personal experiences with God.[33]

The ultimate goal of prayer is love—a love between the person and God which does not absorb him or her, but which enables one to love others more maturely and more deeply. The balance between the inner and outer directedness is essential.

Otherwise, we find persons glorying in spiritual things and forgetting what real love is about. Some immature persons do mistake and misunderstand detachment from the world, and develop a neurotic fear of the physical and sensual in the world. Consequently, they label everything that is natural or pertaining to the body as evil.[34] Our bodies, our senses and our passions are vessels of wholeness and holiness. As Paul says, our bodies are temples of the Holy Spirit (1 Cor 6:19).

So, the Christian life is not a life divided between times for action and relationships and times for contemplation. Mature social action and relationships are ways of contemplation, and real contemplation is the core of love, relationships and Christian social action.[35] Henri Nouwen says that if our desire for silence and prayer is not born out of concern for others in the world, we will soon become bored in our spiritual life. On the other hand, some people have developed the idea that, for the Christian, being present to people in all their needs is their primary vocation. The Bible does not support this. Jesus' primary concern was to be obedient to his Father; only then did it become clear to him what his task was in relationship with people. "Only in God does our neighbor become a neighbor, rather than an infringement upon our autonomy."[36]

Jung maintained that the best insurance for a safe journey inward is to find fellowship in the outer world, in warm and intimate relationships that are growing and developing in love. There is no way that we can help other people become open to relationships with their fellow human beings and with God, except through our expression of love to them. Otherwise, human beings will remain fortresses that may be conquered and brought to subjection, but not open for creative relationships.[37] So love and relationships are the modes, the way in which we live out and manifest our Christian spirituality.

> When we have found the anchor places for our lives in our own center, we can be free to let others enter into the space created for them and allow them to dance their own dance, sing their own song and speak their own language without fear.[38]

Dreams—Inner Wisdom

One of the most important contributions of Jungians in regard to a mature understanding of the human personality, has been pinpointing dreams as meaningful instruments of wisdom for our lives and growth. Dreams are primary points of contact with the unconscious, and as such they put us in touch with not only the wisdom of our inner selves, but also the wisdom of the human race as a whole, and the wisdom of God, in whose image we were created.

The works of John Sanford and Morton Kelsey articulate most effectively the significance of dreams in the context of personal and spiritual growth. At the level of dreams, psychology and religion are inseparable. Sanford says that it is the realm of the spiritual world, including dreams, which "carries to man's consciousness a revelation of the underlying meaning of life, and therefore of God."[39] God is the inner source of our life and energies, speaking to us through our dreams, through our relationships and through the events of our lives.[40] Dreams are a manifestation of God's voice, God's wisdom, to human beings. They remind us that we are "not the masters but the servants" of the God within us.[41]

Our dreams are instruments of personality wholeness and integration. Jung discovered that at the basis of our dreams there is a religious process. The function of dreams is one of reconciling (a feminine function) ourselves to our deepest center and to God's purpose within us.[42] Our dreams can be thought of as reproductions of our inner life situation. Our own person in the dream represents the ego (our conscious self). The other various characters in the dream generally represent other aspects of ourselves.[43] The unconscious chooses symbols from our daily life experience to represent hidden aspects of our personality.

In interpreting dreams, it is important to make note of the mood which accompanies them, as well as the real life events which preceded them. We may have as many as five or six dreams on a given night; they tend to occur every ninety minute period, or so. Dreams in a series can be tremendously insightful tools for understanding a particular stage of our growth. Most Jungians recommend writing our dreams down in a personal journal, and more will be said about journal writing later in this work.

Encounter with Darkness

The spiritual growth journey inevitably involves encounter with evil. The reason why it does is not completely understood by anyone, and I would be very skeptical of anyone who attempted to minimize the importance of evil or to give a simplistic explanation of it. The reality of the existence of evil must be wrestled with in developing a mature spirituality. It is not within the scope of this work to give an extensive discourse on the nature of evil. For our purpose, it must suffice to point out three manifestations of the phenomenon of evil which are important in developing a personal spirituality: (a) the evil in ourselves; (b) the role of suffering; (c) evil as a real and separate spiritual entity.

Henri Nouwen, in his work *The Wounded Healer*, points out that in order to develop a spirituality and to create space for God in our lives, we must be willing to look into the "dark corners of our own house."[44] In ancient times, once the individual arrived at the temple, he/she had to undergo rites of confession and purification. It is evident to us that many contemporary Christians have forgotten the importance of confession for developing a mature spirituality.

In the language of Jungian psychology we call this dealing with the shadow, the inferior, unwanted part of our life and personality. Our tendency is to resist seeing the shadow, because this is not possible without experiencing pain.[45] However, Sanford points out that in spite of the darkness of the shadow, he/she seems close to God. He maintains that when we begin to wrestle with our shadow, we find ourselves—like Jacob—somehow wrestling with God.[46] Nouwen compares spiritual life to making prints from negatives; just as "the dark forests make us speak of the open fields," new life is born out of the pains of the old. He reminds us that we cannot bypass the pain and expect to get to the other side.[47]

This brings us to the next aspect, the role of suffering which always, ultimately, will remain a mystery. However, we can draw some encouragement from the suggestion that God may permit suffering and evil so that life will not get so comfortable for us that we fall psychologically and spiritually asleep. In the words of Sanford:

> Looked at purely clinically, the journey through the wilderness appears to be a sickness or a breakdown; looked at spiritually, it may be an initiation or rite of passage we must undergo, in order that a change in consciousness may be brought about.[48]

In the New Testament when Jesus speaks of faith, he is speaking of the capacity of a person to affirm life in spite of what life may bring and even in the face of darkness (Mk 9:25).

Jacob's experience in the Old Testament is of paramount importance for the Christian. As we wrestle with suffering in our own personal experience, no matter how dark or frightening it becomes, we must refuse to let it go until we discover its meaning. Then we can come through the struggle to the other side reborn. If we retreat we cannot be transformed at all.[49] The wound Jacob received is the mark a person carries who has encountered this deep spiritual and psychological reality. It is a way of saying that someone who encounters and wrestles with suffering can never go back and be the kind of person he/she was before. It can be a lonely experience to be marked by God in this way, because one is forced to recognize one's uniqueness and difference from others who have not had a similar experience.[50]

Finally, not realizing the power of evil as a real and separate reality can result, especially for the Christian, in utter destruction. From an experiential point of view, evil may be described as the power which works for dissociation; it exists specifically whenever a part seeks to take over the whole.[51] From a spiritual standpoint, the object of evil is to separate us from God, while from a psychological standpoint, evil results in the disintegration of the human personality. Morton Kelsey in his latest book, *Discernment*, discusses the nature and function of evil from a theological and psychological standpoint. For our purposes here, I merely wish to remind the reader of the importance of wrestling with and understanding this issue in the context of Christian spirituality. Too many of us, myself included, have dismissed this reality in the past, simply because it does not fit in with our intellectual understanding of the theology of creation and the overall purposes of a merciful and loving God, according to our own human logical perspective. Like the existence of God, the existence of evil, as a separate spiritual entity, is a phenomenon which cannot be proven to anyone. It is a matter of faith and of personal experience. It is extremely difficult to articulate in a meaningful way to another person who has not had this kind of experience. It pertains to the discussion of spirituality because it works toward dissociation, instead of integration and wholeness, of the person and his/her relationships with God and others.

Celebration and Community

Celebration and community are the context of mature Christian spirituality. This is the phenomenon which we call the church, the ultimate and corporate expression of the kingdom of God on earth. As Christians, we are all called to celebration and community. There is no such thing as a Christian outside of the church. By church we mean the organic phenomenon of the people of God, not the institutional church or a particular tradition or denomination. The Scriptures indicate that we cannot be whole and mature Christians without relating to a faith community. The Christian community is the nurturing context which feeds and nourishes us, and through which we give a unique expression to our faith. It does this through the sacraments and through worship.

Kelsey points out that in sacramental religious experience the divine comes into focus directly through an element of the outer physical world.[52] We humans need these tangible and concrete focal points of God's saving presence with us. It was Carl Jung who noted that the Christian church structure offered the finest system of psychotherapy man ever had.[53] The two most vital rituals of the Christian church are the sacraments of the Lord's supper and baptism.

The sacraments and rituals of the church give us an immediate contact with the historical base of Christianity. In and through the sacraments we participate in the realities that have been revealed at one point in history, and which continue to be revealed within each one of us. The sacrament of baptism commits the individual to a new way of life, and it marks his/her entry into the Christian family and fellowship. The sacrament of baptism in the New Testament is the church's celebration of the conscious choice of spiritual rebirth of which we spoke earlier in this chapter.

In the sacrament of the Lord's supper, we are nurtured in a concrete way by Christ's gift of self. Here the ordinary food of Jesus' time, the bread and the wine, are used to express the totality of his gift of self and his continuing presence, among and within us. In receiving his body and blood we know that he gives himself to us over and over again. We do not just remember something that happened at one point in time, but we are transformed each time we receive it by his life and his love.

The sacraments, according to Kelsey, provide us with a base of reality for the inward journey. They keep us in touch with the historical reality of Christianity, the way God entered into the world in Christ. They also keep us in touch with the importance of our physical nature, both in itself and as means through which God can continue to break through to us and our world. The sacraments also make us realize how important the simplest, most physical acts can be as ways of allowing God to reveal himself to us. Commonplace actions like touching, bathing and eating can become important ways of opening our lives to him[54] who touched people as he healed them, washed the feet of his disciples and ate with them at Passover celebrations, weddings, etc.

The power of the sacraments and ritual celebrations in the church is that they enable us to affirm in a concrete way our present conditions. They connect us with our history—our past. They fill us with a sense of openness and expectation about the present and the future, and they give us a sense of hope.[55] The most meaningful context in which to realize these special experiences is in community. The context of a Christian community protects and affirms our prayer life. It enables us to grow and flower, because it provides us with enough support to take the risk to reach out and look beyond our private and individual needs.[56] It helps to make us ready for a life of ministry, for our ultimate vocation. More will be said about this in the next chapter.

Henri Nouwen says that St. Thomas the apostle, who was skeptical of the report of the resurrection of the Lord, remained faithful to the community. It was in that community that the Lord appeared to him and strengthened his faith. In times of doubt or unbelief, the community can carry us along. It can offer on our behalf what we overlook, and it can be the context in which we may recognize the Lord again.[57]

Becoming part of a faith community requires a commitment to trust and obedience on the part of the individual. It is not a matter of adapting and molding ourselves to the community, in the sense of conformity and losing our identity. But it does require a willingness to listen to others and to be accountable to the particular group with which we choose to affiliate. In this way, the Christian community is a valuable instrument in developing a balanced spirituality.

In this chapter the basic elements of Christian spirituality have been identified with reference to contemporary Jungian theologians: beginning with a personal and conscious choice about the identity of Jesus, fostering a condition of creative solitude in order to develop a prayer life, learning the role of love and relationships, looking at dreams as a source of inner wisdom and wholeness, encountering various manifestations of evil, and viewing celebration within a Christian community as the nurturing context for a mature spirituality. In the next chapter a brief overview of classical approaches to Christian spirituality will be presented and examined with regard to their compatibility with the feminine mode.

Notes

1. Henri Nouwen, *The Genesee Diary* (New York: Doubleday & Co., 1976), p. 21.

2. Elizabeth Boyden Howes, *Intersection and Beyond* (San Francisco: Guild for Psychological Studies, 1971), p. 118.

3. Elizabeth Boyden Howes and Sheila Moon, *Man the Choicemaker* (Philadelphia: Westminster Press, 1973), p. 209.

4. John Sanford, *The Kingdom Within* (New York: J.B. Lippincott Co., 1970), pp. 51–52.

5. *Ibid.*, p. 63.

6. *Idem, Healing and Wholeness* (New York: Paulist Press, 1971), p. 71.

7. Henri Nouwen, *Creative Ministry* (New York: Doubleday & Co., 1971), p. 10.

8. Morton Kelsey, *The Other Side of Silence* (New York: Paulist Press, 1976), p. 97.

9. Henri Nouwen, *Reaching Out* (New York: Doubleday & Co., 1975), pp. 22–23.

10. *Idem, Out of Solitude* (Notre Dame: Ave Maria Press, 1974), p. 14.

11. Morton Kelsey, *Myth, History, and Faith* (New York: Paulist Press, 1974), pp. 152–153.

12. Henri Nouwen, *Out of Solitude*, p. 26.

13. Morton Kelsey, *The Other Side of Silence*, p. 98.

14. Henri Nouwen, *Out of Solitude*, p. 14.

15. *Ibid.*, p. 61.

16. John Sanford, *Healing and Wholeness*, p. 133.

17. Henri Nouwen, *Reaching Out*, p. 88.

18. *Ibid.*, p. 89.

19. *Idem, The Genesee Diary*, p. 108.

20. *Idem, Out of Solitude*, p. 55.

21. *Idem, The Genesee Diary*, p. 184.

22. *Ibid.*, p. 169.

23. *Ibid.*, p. 118.

24. *Ibid.*, p. 120.

25. *Ibid.*, p. 22.

26. *Idem, Reaching Out*, p. 95.

27. Morton Kelsey, *The Other Side of Silence*, pp. 21–22.

28. Henri Nouwen, *The Genesee Diary*, p. 121.

29. *Idem, Reaching Out*, p. 107.

30. *Idem, The Genesee Diary*, p. 56.

31. Morton Kelsey, *The Other Side of Silence*, p. 139.

32. Henri Nouwen, *The Genesee Diary*, p. 123.

33. Morton Kelsey, *The Other Side of Silence*, pp. 62–63.

34. *Ibid.*, pp. 98–99.

35. Henri Nouwen, *Creative Ministry*, p. 87.

36. *Idem, The Living Reminder* (New York: Seabury Press, 1977), pp. 30–31.

37. Morton Kelsey, *The Other Side of Silence*, p. 64.

38. Henri Nouwen, *The Wounded Healer* (New York: Doubleday & Co., 1972), p. 93.

39. John Sanford, *Dreams, God's Forgotten Language* (New York: J.B. Lippincott Co., 1968), p. 9.

40. *Ibid.*, p. 215.

41. *Ibid.*, p. 214.

42. *Ibid.*, p. 200.

43. *Ibid.*, pp. 127–128.

44. Henri Nouwen, *The Wounded Healer*, p. 38.

45. John Sanford, *Healing and Wholeness*, p. 57.

46. *Idem, Dreams, God's Forgotten Language*, p. 132.

47. Henri Nouwen, *Reaching Out*, pp. 10–11.

48. John Sanford, *The Man Who Wrestled with God* (King of Prussia: Religious Publishing Co., 1974), p. 27.

49. *Ibid.*, p. 44.

50. *Ibid.*

51. *Idem, The Kingdom Within*, p. 138.

52. Morton Kelsey, *The Other Side of Silence*, p. 131.

53. *Idem, Myth, Mystery, and Faith*, p. 171.

54. *Idem, The Other Side of Silence*, p. 195.

55. Henri Nouwen, *Creative Ministry*, p. 93.

56. *Idem, Reaching Out*, p. 109.

57. *Idem, The Genesee Diary*, p. 40.

4

Classical Approaches to the Spiritual Life

The purpose of this chapter is to examine, briefly, several classical approaches to Christian spirituality with regard to their compatibility with the feminine mode and mature spirituality.

Introduction to Mysticism

Evelyn Underhill, in her book *Practical Mysticism*, compares the mystic with the artist. For her, the artist is no more and no less than a contemplative who has learned to express himself/herself and who tells his/her love in color, speech or sound. Similarly, the mystic is an artist of a special kind, who tries to express something of the revelation he/she has received.[1]

In order to aid our understanding of mysticism, let us review the three sources from which comes our knowledge of God (according to Evelyn Underhill): (1) the natural world, which we call natural theology, (2) history and Christian revelation, referred to as dogmatic theology, and (3) the individual's direct spiritual experience, known as mystical theology. To be whole Christians we need something of all three. But prayer (mystical theology) is the means by which we enter into the other two realms.[2] As noted in Chapter 1, it is not by science that we learn to know life, nor is it by the methods of the intellect that we learn to know God; it is through our own personal experience.[3]

The overall focus of the mystic, and ideally of any Christian, is aimed primarily at union with God. The mystical life is active and purposeful in character and is nothing less than the union of the spirit of an individual with God, who is the Spirit-center of the universe.[4]

Traditionally, the mystical way involves three stages: purgation (or purification), illumination and union. This format was first used by the neo-Platonists, and it was borrowed from them by earlier Christian writers on the spiritual life. It describes, in general terms, the way in which the spirit of the mystic develops. In the next chapter of this work, we will develop contemporary aspects of the spiritual life analogous to these presented here.

Purgation refers to the purification of one's character, i.e., confession, cleansing, admitting one's sinfulness. It entails a certain attitude of detachment regarding material and worldly values. In other words, the person relates to things and people in a non-possessive manner, viewing them as special gifts from God. Here the individual is primarily active, i.e., he/she is consciously making an effort to develop certain attitudes and he/she is encouraged by God's grace. It is a stage of making oneself ready for a more committed and intimate relationship with God.

The stage of illumination refers to a growing sense of peace and certitude about God, as one who loved us first. Here the person experiences an increasing awareness of the values of human existence and the universe, in the light of God's kingdom. His/her perspective merges more and more into Jesus' perspective, as presented in the New Testament, and he/she also experiences a greater willingness to surrender his/her will to him.

The third stage of union has to do with an overall harmony between one's being and will and God himself, that is, an even fuller integration of the Christian way, the way of love. This attitude makes us more effective instruments of God. Underhill talks about it as a union so completely established that it persists unbroken for long periods of time, among the distractions and difficulties of the world. It often drives those who achieve it to renounce the private joys of contemplation in order to dedicate themselves more fully to work for God in the world.[5] The latter is contrary to the popular and mistaken conception of the mystic in our day, but it is self-evident in the lives of the saints.

As we now review the spirituality of individual mystics, it is important for the reader to remember that these were each unique persons who lived within a particular community, in a particular environment and period of history, and it is within this context that their contribution must be evaluated.

Teresa of Avila and Ignatius of Loyola were chosen because they both developed systematic and comprehensive approaches to the growth of the spiritual life which are still greatly respected and treasured today. I was curious about the differences of emphases from a masculine and feminine perspective. The fact that they were both Catholic and Spanish mystics, who wrote at the time of the Counter-Reformation era, was an arbitrary choice and of no special significance, per se, to the subject of this work.

Evelyn Underhill and Thomas Merton provide two modern examples of Protestant and Catholic writing, respectively, in the area of Christian spirituality, whose extensive works have been among the most noted in the last century. In the last section of this chapter, differences between Catholic and Protestant spirituality are summarized regarding the feminine mode of being.

Teresa of Avila's Seven Dwellings

As Teresa of Avila struggled with the task of writing about the spiritual life and prayer, she received a vision in which she pictured a crystal globe in the shape of a castle, containing seven "moradas" (most writers have translated this term as "mansions"; I have chosen the word "dwellings," because it is much closer to the Spanish meaning, in my opinion). In the seventh and innermost dwelling was Jesus, "the King of Glory," illuminating them all, and the nearer to the center, the stronger and more brilliant the light. Outside these dwellings everything was foul and dark, infested with venomous creatures.[6]

Teresa's intuition and creative imagination pictured the spiritual life and prayer as a process of illumination, or a movement toward God's (self or) light (see Jn 1:4–5; 1 Jn 1:5), in the person of Jesus. In her mind, the seven dwellings provide a progression of resting places which lead us home, to the ultimate and final place of oneness or wholeness, union with Christ. Each Christian's movement toward the light is unique and different. The movement itself is not discrete and linear, but it is better described as spiral. The seven dwellings are meant to describe interdependent stages of growth in the life of prayer and our faith relationship with God.

The seven dwellings can be viewed in terms of two phases. The first phase includes the first three dwellings. Here, God intervenes in our prayer life in a natural way, through our cooperation with his grace. In a sense, we are primarily active in these stages, making a conscious effort to grow and develop certain attitudes. Jordan Aumann, a Dominican priest who has written about Teresa's model, says that the first three mansions are like ante-rooms, and there are many of these. Most Christians remain in these and never go any further. They live generally in the state of grace, but they do the minimum required in the Christian life. (It should be remembered that those living habitually in serious sin are considered by Teresa to be outside the seven dwellings, in the darkness.)

The second phase of the spiritual progression includes the fourth through the seventh dwellings, where we adopt a more receptive posture and we are more open to God's grace and his spirit working in us.[7] Both phases require times of solitude and the attitudes of detachment and humility, as well as loving relationships with others and sharing with a faith community. It can be said that the feminine mode of being predominates more in the second phase, rather than in the first, because of the relative emphasis upon a receptive vs. active attitude.

Some writers have referred to these two phases of prayer, or the spiritual life, as the ascetical (active) and the mystical (receptive). The following is an outline of the potential growth of our prayer life, according to traditional Catholic spirituality. It is presented here because it will facilitate an understanding of Teresa's model and context for the prayer life and our growth in holiness.

Since our Western minds find most of this foreign, this material is arranged in charts in the following pages in order to summarize the characteristics and behaviors which generally accompany each stage of prayer, or "dwelling," along with the predominant virtue or theme corresponding to each. The chart is merely a tool seeking to present an overall picture of Teresa's model, although, in practice, these are not as discrete as they appear in the outline. More details concerning these can be found in Teresa's book, *Interior Castle,* and in Aumann's tapes regarding the same.[9]

Given Teresa's model, one would surmise that very few persons arrive at the last stages of the seven dwellings in their lifetime. They are gifts from God, dependent upon his grace, and also upon our receptivity and willingness to undertake the spiritual journey. Nevertheless, Teresa's model is quite a challenge to expand our growth and potential in the spiritual life and in prayer.

Teresa believed that union with God through love was much more intimate than through knowledge, and that action and contemplation were not at odds with each other, but had a complementary relationship instead:

> . . . what is the good . . . of being deeply recollected in solitude . . . promising our Lord to do wonders in His service, if when we come out of prayer, the least thing makes us do the exact opposite.[10]

The wisdom of Teresa's model of the life of prayer is that, through symbol and imagination, she conceptualized a biblical description of the spiritual life as a dynamic process, which is unique for each person and yet universal. She managed to capture the complementarity of its masculine and feminine dimensions, which are both necessary, focusing on the person of Christ as the ultimate end.

The Way of Ignatius of Loyola

While Teresa focused primarily upon the life of prayer, the spirituality of Ignatius is of a more concrete and practical nature. It provides specifications for a four-week period of spiritual self-examination and lifelong commitment to Christ. The week period is meant to be flexible and the spiritual guide or mentor is

ASCETICAL—ACTIVE PHASE

1. *Vocal Prayer*—prayer said out loud

2. *Mental Prayer*—quiet prayer

   (a) Meditation

       i. discursive meditation—a conscious focusing on the mysteries of the life experience of Christ on this earth.

       ii. affective meditation—a more open-ended approach to meditation where we allow our mind and "heart" to focus on our relationship and experience of God as it will, and where we have awareness of a feeling of love and closeness with God.

   (b) Acquired Recollection—called prayer of "simplicity"; the faculties and attention are focused on God even more intently, and the individual allows God to take even more of a lead in the direction of his/her prayer life.

MYSTICAL—RECEPTIVE PHASE

1. *Infused Recollection or Contemplation*—a state of greater intimacy with God in prayer, e.g., the Jesus Prayer, charismatic prayer, etc.

2. *Prayer of Quiet*—the human will is totally surrendered to God; there is a deep sense of peace and serenity and joy in his presence.

3. *Prayer of Union*—like Paul ("no longer I, but Christ lives in me"), a transformation has taken place at a deep spiritual level. The following are degrees of such:

   (a) simple union with God;

   (b) ecstatic union with God;

   (c) conforming union with God;

   (d) transforming union with God.[8]

CHART #1

TERESA'S MODEL FOR THE LIFE OF PRAYER:

(Stages 1 & 2)

Dwellings	Type of Prayer	Examples of Characteristics/Behaviors	Suggested Virtue/Theme(s)
First	Vocal Prayer	a. saying prayers out loud b. thinking about God once in a while c. beginning meditation occasionally d. making a retreat once a year	Humility
Second	Meditation	a. cultivating a taste for prayer b. being more attentive in prayer c. being attracted to the things of God and the Church d. associating with other devout Christians e. prayer becoming more of a priority f. realizing the need for the attitude of detachment g. wanting to grow in holiness h. delighting in prayer because it is pleasant, but giving up when discouraged	Detachment

CHART #2

CONTINUATION OF TERESA'S MODEL
(Stages 3 & 4)

Dwellings	Type of Prayer	Examples of Characteristics/Behaviors	Suggested Virtue/Theme(s)
Third	Acquired Recollection	a. giving witness to virtues of the Christian life b. being recognized by others as a devout Christian c. feeling more secure in God's love d. trying to avoid even small occasions of sin e. making regular acts of confession f. making spontaneous acts of charity and love g. spending more time in prayer h. having some dry periods but not being discouraged i. the intellect and reason still predominating in prayer life	Charity
Fourth	Contemplation	a. being less active and more receptive b. being freed from fear of hell or punishment c. being less attached to the world d. being aware of the kingdom of God from within	Self-Surrender

CHART #3

CONTINUATION OF TERESA'S MODEL
(Stages 5 – 7)

Dwellings	Type of Prayer	Examples of Characteristics/Behaviors	Suggested Virtue/Theme(s)
Fifth	Simple Union	a. being more intimate with God b. divine presence of God permeating individual c. having many trials d. having a clearer awareness of the relationship between contemplation and action	Intimacy with God
Sixth	Conforming Union	a. having an even more intense relationship with God b. having periods of crises and sometimes being unable to pray c. sometimes having visions and locutions from God	Greater Intimacy, Perseverance
Seventh	Transforming Union	a. being like Paul: "no longer I, but Christ lives in me" b. having sometimes visions of Jesus c. achieving a high degree of self-forgetfulness and abandonment to the will of God d. doing everything for the glory of God	Perfect "Oneness" with God

encouraged to consider each person's unique needs, when giving direction, in order to accomplish the desired growth.

In the first week, one meditates upon his/her own sinfulness; in the second week, on the life of Christ and the call to serve him; in the third week, on Christ's passion and death; and in the fourth week, on the risen and glorified Christ.[11]

The Spiritual Exercises begin with the consideration of a basic life question: "What is man's final end?" (akin to "What is the meaning of life?"—see Chapter 1). The first week is also largely focused on sin as a conscious choice to separate ourselves from God through a review of Adam and Eve's sin, the angels' sin, and the sin of all humans. Its purpose is to pinpoint humanity's dependence on God and our need for the redeeming love of Christ.[12]

Ignatius gives practical suggestions on how to review the sinfulness of our lives. But the Jesuit John English, in his contemporary approach to Ignatian spirituality, talks about discerning one's basic disorder (sin), rather than a list of sins.[13] For example, in asking "What in my life is enslaving me? What is interfering with my freedom and with a total surrendering of myself to God?"[14] English argues that searching out one's basic disorder enables one to increase his/her ability to love and avoid serious sin.[15] The result is greater wholeness. He suggests that by the end of the first week the person should resemble the sinful woman in Luke's Gospel who washes the Lord's feet. She comes emptying herself, and he loves her and bestows upon her the ability to love. The Lord is her Savior and lifts her out of her helplessness.[16] Identifying and confessing our sinfulness (or basic disorder or neurosis) frees us spiritually and psychologically to consider the call to serve Christ which is the focus of the second week.

The primary aim of the second week is to persuade the individual to an intimate knowledge and love of the person of Jesus. This is brought about by a series of meditations on Jesus' private and public life and on the kingdom of God. Other meditations, such as those on the two standards of living and the three classes of men, etc., are aimed at leading the person to make a decision to follow Christ and join in working for the development of his kingdom on this earth.[17]

English takes from Roustang several subjective and objective criteria which are helpful in making a decision about our spiritual life and commitment to Christ. The subjective criteria from which we can discern guidance are the affective experiences of disquiet or anxiety vs. delight and peace—e.g., joy is the principal sign of the presence of Jesus, according to English, and an overall sense of harmony within us. Among the objective criteria identified are an attitude of love and a willingness to follow Christ, and a subordination to the Holy Spirit, operating within the Christian community.[18] Another way of saying this is that the latter are external indications which help us discern the degree of commitment of a person to Christ.

The second week of the Ignatian retreat culminates in a decision by the individual about his/her state of life, (cf. Jung's view about the relationship between one's life purpose and identity and one's vocation, in Chapter 2). At this point, English reminds us that Christ was tempted at two moments of great decisions—first at the beginning of his public life, and then at the moment of acceptance of the Father's will in the Garden of Gethsemane.[19] It is essential for a Christian to know that temptations can be expected, especially right after the initial commitment to Christ and later when we get close to engaging freely in a life of ministry. Discernment plays a particularly important role here. At the end of the book on the Spiritual Exercises, Ignatius provides a number of rules for discernment designed to assist the individual about the temptations or obstacles which may accompany his/her decision. More will be said about discerning God's will for our lives in the next chapter.

The third and fourth weeks comprise, together, a movement beyond the self. Identifying ourselves with Christ as a human being, and contemplating his gift of self in his suffering and death, in the third week we are confirmed and given an impetus in our decision to follow him.[20] In the fourth week we are led to adopt the attitude of self-surrender of Christ himself. This posture is particularly consistent with the feminine mode of openness and receptivity.

Later, in the fourth week, Ignatius leads retreatants into meditations on the risen life of Christ. Through the resurrection we are freed and enabled to love unselfishly, to see beyond the obstacles of our lives, because our hope and strength comes from him whose story does not end in death and desolation but in life, restoring all creation to himself.[21] "Where our love overflows in deeds, we become aware of the presence of LOVE, which is Christ himself."[22] Our love, in turn, frees others and the end result is a unity of purpose—ours with Christ in working for the kingdom.

The Ignatian way is a thorough one. It takes the Christian from an awareness of his/her sinfulness and its forgiveness (first week); through a process of examination of lifestyle alternatives and a conscious choice to follow Christ (second week); which leads to an attitude of self-surrender, patterned after Christ's own suffering and death (third week); in order to reap the fruits of the resurrection—peace, joy and love—in working for the kingdom (fourth week).

Ignatius may be difficult to understand for the beginner of the Christian walk. His approach is very structured and very masculine. But, translated into a contemporary context, it can be a helpful tool for the person who is serious about making a lifelong commitment to Christ. Retreats, as comprehensive as these, are most profitable when they are made with a spiritual guide; more will be said about the latter later in this work.

The Ignatian emphasis is masculine, i.e., upon what humans can do, as opposed to what God does with our receptive cooperation. It depends heavily on (what Jung called) active imagination for the meditations suggested. Yet, it is comprised of significant feminine components at several junctures, such as: the attitude of self-surrender, necessary to accept God's will for one's life; the receptive posture required for the meditations to be meaningful; becoming one with Christ in his purpose for the kingdom, etc. Now we turn to a more modern approach to Christian spirituality, in the work of Evelyn Underhill.

The Spirituality of Evelyn Underhill

Underhill's understanding of spirituality is one which does not require a special monastic career outside of the world. She maintains that spirituality is a part of every person's life, and until one realizes it he/she is not a complete human being.[23] She sees it as an educative process, reaching a level of understanding which involves the development and training of a layer of consciousness largely underutilized[24] (see Chapter 1). Preparation for developing the spiritual life requires the discipline of our attention, the simplification of our lifestyles, and the reorientation of our affections and our will.[25]

In her book *Practical Mysticism*, Evelyn Underhill talks about a progression in prayer which includes recollection, meditation and three forms of contemplation. She defines recollection as the subjection of the attention to the control of the will. It is a voluntary concentration of the mind.[26] Meditation, then, is a halfway house between thinking and contemplating.[27] We begin to allow God's spirit to lead us, but we still exercise conscious control of our attention. The beginning of meditation for most Christians is a very difficult period, because most of us are not accustomed to being still and quiet, which demonstrates how unruly and ill-educated is our attention.[28] Our task is to remain patient and faithful in its practice, day after day, bringing our attention back to the focus of our meditation each time.

Our life experience is often so crowded and disjointed that it hinders the practice of meditation. As we simplify our life perspective, Underhill maintains that we will discover something within us which we can recollect or gather up. This experience brings us to a deeper level of awareness of our own existence: "You will, in fact, know your own soul for the first time. . . ."[29] This deeper level of awareness marks the beginning of contemplation:

> You have discovered your inmost sanctuary . . . you recognize it as the true self, whose existence you take for granted, but whom you have only known in its scattered manifestations.[30]

Most people think of contemplation as a lofty and easy activity. On the contrary, the journey to contemplation is a lonely and arduous excursion, where few can really bear to see themselves face to face. It requires a kind of self-confrontation (see Chapter 1), which inevitably leads the person to a sense of awe before God and a deep sorrowfulness about his/her sinfulness. Here is the place where conversion takes place in the most drastic sense. One is compelled to take up a new attitude toward oneself and all other things.[31]

In the first form of contemplation, the individual rediscovers the world, seeing God in every aspect of creation. Underhill says that we discover a new relationship of profound significance between ourselves and everything in God's universe,[32] i.e., our fraternal link with all living things. (The reader who may be interested in pursuing in further depth this aspect of contemplation may turn to the spirituality of St. Francis of Assisi and/or that of Meister Eckhart.) This aspect of contemplation is extremely important in the context of love, which, according to Underhill, contemplation teaches. In contemplation, we experience the thing itself directly, instead of thinking about it. It is an experience of sensation without thought.[33] When we love someone maturely, we can accept him/her as he/she is, without expectations or conditions.

In the second form of contemplation the person finds himself/herself emptied and freed, in a place stripped of all the machinery of thought, where he/she can just be. It is as if we had a newly discovered space of our own. Underhill describes the experience as a sense of finding one's ultimate place in the world:

> ... the condition ... which some call nakedness of spirit—a state of consciousness in which all the workings of reason fail ... there you will observe that you have entered into an intense and vivid silence. . . . Yet in spite of the darkness that enfolds you . . . you are sure that it is well to be there.[34]

In the third form of contemplation all that happens seems without effort on our part. It is like coming to a country described by St. Augustine as "no mere vision, but a home." We are to let ourselves go and cease all conscious or anxious striving, simply being there with our "doors flung wide open towards God." As we initially go into that place, we may feel lost or bewildered for a while, because we have never been there before. We are like strangers in a foreign land. We may experience confusion, darkness and even boredom, but, if we are faithful and we do not allow fear or restlessness to get in the way, and if we also persevere, we come to the place where our human spirit can dwell in a most intimate way with the very Spirit of God.[35] This experience can be enjoyed by all Christians who wish to experience a deeper and fuller spiritual life.

Underhill sees the religious contemplative as one who is by nature a missionary as well. The vision which the person has achieved in contemplation is a vision of an intensely loving heart. Since love cannot keep itself to itself, it urges the person to tell the good news of the Gospel to others.[36] She also maintains that the prevalent notion that spirituality and politics have nothing to do with one another is the exact opposite of the truth. The spiritual life has everything to do with politics. It means that certain convictions about God and the world become the moral and spiritual imperatives of our life.[37] The spiritual life is simply a life in which all that we do comes from the center, where we are anchored in God himself.[38]

> Only when the conviction . . . that the demand of the Spirit, however inconvenient, comes first and is first . . . will those objectionable voices die down, which have a way of . . . drowning all the quieter voices.[39]

Underhill's spirituality is a holistic approach to God, whereby each person, through discipline and simplicity, can enter into a new relationship with God and with the rest of creation. The Christian, approaching this place within, discovers a new identity and a deeper intimacy with God. This level of intimacy, this love experience, urges the Christian to share and practice with others the truth that he/she has found.

Thomas Merton and Holiness

Thomas Merton understood the spiritual life as a kind of dialectic between ideals and reality. In other words, we become holy, not by realizing a universal standard of perfection, but, by responding to God's call and his love for us, which he addresses to each person, within the particular limitations and circumstances of his/her life and vocation.[40]

Holiness is not something that we acquire outside of Christ in order to qualify for union with him. It is the work of Christ himself (of his Spirit) living in us by faith.[41] It is a process. Growing in holiness does not mean that we put aside our human nature, but it is just the opposite. Merton believed that before a person can become a saint, he/she must first of all be a person in all the humanity and fragility of man's actual condition. Christianity is greatly hindered by persons seeking to become more spiritual than anyone while they are still emotionally immature. Merton warns us that if we do not seek to be fully human, we will never be able to understand Jesus as a man, who was the holiest of all the saints: "Sanctity is not a matter of being less human, but more human than other men."[42]

Merton believed that we are suffering more from the distortion and underdevelopment of our deepest human tendencies than from a super-abundance of animal instincts.[43] This is very important, because many Christians in their immature efforts to grow spiritually suppress their emotions and become neurotic instead of saintly. Merton's stance was that human nature is not evil, neither is all pleasure wrong, nor are all spontaneous desires selfish. For him, the doctrine of original sin does not mean that human nature has been completely corrupted, nor that man's freedom is always inclined to sin. In his words:

> Man is neither a devil nor an angel. He is not a pure spirit, but a being of flesh and spirit, who is subject to error and malice, but is basically inclined to seek truth and goodness. He is indeed a sinner, but his heart responds to love and grace.[44]

At times Christian traditions have given evil and Satan more credit than they deserve.

Most Christians have a very nebulous understanding of grace. Merton emphasized that grace builds on human nature, not by suppressing instinct, but by healing and transforming it. Therefore, the Christian who wants to follow Christ must not do so by imposing a crude and violent control on his/her emotions, but by letting grace form and develop his/her emotional life in the service of love.[45]

Some Christians think of grace as a kind of mysterious substance which is furnished to us by God—"something like fuel for a supernatural engine," says Merton. We regard it as a kind of spiritual gasoline which we need to make our journey to God. This view is terribly mistaken. Grace is not something with which we perform good works and attain God. It is God's very presence and action within us. It is the sanctifying energy of God, acting dynamically in our lives.[46]

In the New Testament, Paul asks us to walk (live) not according to the flesh, but according to the spirit. The flesh is the generic term, not for bodily life (since the body, along with the soul is sanctified by the Holy Spirit), but for mundane life, according to Merton. The flesh includes not just sensuality and licentiousness, but also worldly conformism and actions based on human respect and social preoccupation. Merton says that we obey the flesh when we follow the norms of prejudice, complacency, bigotry, group pride, superstition, ambition and greed.[47] Therefore, to reject the world is not to reject people, or society, or the creatures of God, or the works of humans, but to reject the perverted standards which make humans misuse and spoil a good creation and ruin their own lives.[48] To sum up, it is in the context of a strong and powerful affirmation of our human nature that Merton spoke of holiness and the spiritual life. Let us look at some specific aspects of contemplative prayer from Merton's perspective.

For Merton, contemplation is the highest expression of human life, because it is the fulfillment of deep capacities in us that God designed not to be fulfilled in any other way.[49] Contemplative prayer takes place in the context of a faith relationship with God.[50] In other words, God elicits a personal call to each individual, through Christ, through whom he has already expressed his deep and personal love to each of us.[51] Our response is, not to love God back but, first, to believe in his love, to consent to it and to open ourselves to it.[52] When we accept and receive God's love, our lives are gradually and, surely, transformed and we begin the journey of communion with him.

At times we Christians become very discouraged in our prayer lives, and we feel very inadequate as we pray. Merton asks us not to be so discouraged, for it is the will to pray that is the essence of prayer, and the desire to find God that really matters.[53] With God, our motivation and intentions matter much more than our performance. Merton believes that we can prepare ourselves for the gift of contemplative prayer by deepening our knowledge and our love of God through the practice of meditation and active forms of prayer.[54]

The practice of meditation teaches us to discipline our minds, memories, and wills in order to become more aware of the presence of God.[55] Some Christians, in their zeal to learn how to meditate, focus too much on the method rather than on prayer itself, and therefore they miss the gift of prayer completely. For Merton, the purpose of a book on meditation is to teach us how to think and not to do the thinking for us. The best thing that beginners in prayer can do—after they have acquired the discipline of mind to concentrate on a subject and to get below the surface of its meaning—is to free their minds and hearts to find God everywhere they go and in all that they do.[56]

A second aspect of preparation, for the gift of contemplative prayer, is an attitude of poverty of heart or detachment.[57] There is a kind of crude materialism (or false detachment) among some devout Christians, which makes them believe that they are to detach themselves from things that please their exterior senses. Merton believes that it is necessary to have a spirit of detachment regarding intellectual and spiritual matters as well.[58] For example, he says that in order to have peace and recollection, we must even let go of the desire for the same, for their own sake:

> . . . desire and seek one thing only, God's will. He will give you recollection and peace, in the middle of labor, conflict and trial.[59]

According to Merton, the ordinary way to contemplative prayer is "through a desert, without trees, without beauty and without water."[60] It is as if we die and are born again to these things. It is important to realize that we do not detach ourselves from things in order to attach ourselves to God, but rather we become detached from ourselves in order to see and use all things in and for God. The detachment from the world, of which we speak, is really detachment from inordinate self-concern.[61] We do not lose our identity, but by making space for the Creator in our lives we find our deepest self.

Solitude is an important condition for the journey to contemplative prayer. Merton distinguishes between true and false solitude. True solitude is the home of the person, as opposed to false solitude, which is the refuge of the individualist. The person, for Merton, is one who is constituted by a unique capacity to love, and the individualist has lost that important perspective and seeks self for its own sake, without concern for others.[62]

An example of such a loss of perspective is the individual who may believe he/she is being faithful in prayer and times of solitude, but who is unable to give up his/her resentment toward another person. In speaking about detachment, Merton says that resentment is among the most difficult, and yet most necessary of renunciations.[63] In his eyes, all forms of sorrow, hardship, pain, unhappiness and ultimately death itself can be traced to an attitude of rebellion or an unwillingness to accept God's love for us,[64] and to dwell upon our unhappy feeling because it is, at least, familiar and safe. This principle is well known to those who have experienced deep healing in their lives, as well as to those who are actively engaged in the healing ministry. Many times people are afraid to be loved, healed and freed from their misery. If unhappiness is all they have ever known, letting go of it can be very threatening.

A safeguard against the false solitude of the individualist is establishing a relationship of accountability to a spiritual director and to a specific Christian community. This sense of accountability is the heart of the principle of obedience, whose root (in Latin) means "responsive listening." Merton, emphasizing obedience and the need for a spiritual director, cautions us against the contemplative who is guided by nobody:

> The most dangerous man in the world . . . He trusts his own visions. He obeys the attractions of an interior voice, but will not listen to other men. He identifies the will of God with anything that makes him feel . . . a big, warm, sweet, interior glow. The sweeter and warmer the feeling is, the more he is convinced of his own infallibility. . . . When you are led by God into the darkness where contemplation is found, you are not able to rest in the false sweetness of your own will.[65]

Finally, Merton, like others, addresses the relationship between interior contemplation and outside activity. These are two aspects of the same love of God. The activity of a contemplative must be born out of his/her contemplation and it must resemble it:

> Everything he does outside of contemplation ought to reflect the luminous tranquility of his interior life. To this end, he will have to look for the same thing in his activity that he finds in contemplation—contact and union with God.[66]

Merton's approach to holiness clearly affirms our humanity. He views contemplative prayer as a gift, which is the ultimate expression of human life. Although he enumerates conditions which foster our readiness for contemplative prayer, he clearly points out that it is God's love which initiates the journey within us, through faith, and it is his love also, manifested through us toward others, which is the ultimate result of our communion with him.

Underhill's and Merton's disciplines are both compatible with the feminine mode. The former emphasizes integration, receptivity and intimacy with God, and the latter focuses upon responsiveness to God's love and acceptance of our humanity, resulting in closer relationships with other human beings.

Protestant and Catholic Spirituality
An Overview

The last section of this chapter is devoted to pinpointing some key differences between practical aspects of Protestant and Catholic spirituality. Christians need to be aware of the richness of the heritage of various Christian traditions. Most of all, we need to consider the differences of emphases as opportunities for learning, instead of obstacles which separate us from each other. The very terms "Protestant" and "Catholic" are extremely inadequate in the light of various denominations, and even among subgroups within these denominations. However, the goal here is not to oversimplify, to caricature or to pass judgment, but to make some general statements about the feminine and masculine modes of being in terms of comparative areas of emphases among Christian traditions.

Douglas Steere, the Quaker theologian, maintained that it is possible to become so concerned with trying to chart the navigational routes most suited for fostering spiritual growth that we will be tempted to forget Augustine's warning: "We come to God by love and not by navigation."[67] It is with this spirit of love that we pursue the following section of this work.

Traditionally, until the renewal occasioned by the Second Vatican Council, Protestant spirituality has laid more emphasis upon the responsibility of the individual than the Roman Catholic perspective. Protestants have been highly sensitive about the Catholic claim that the priest or the institutional Church can stand as an indispensable intermediary for Christians. Protestants, generally, have also emphasized that the mediation of Jesus Christ is the one and only intervention that is required in the Christian faith.[68] The Catholic perspective, in its practice, has generally maintained that the institutional church, through the clergy, and ultimately through the Pope, is the primary interpreter of the truth which is in the Scriptures, regarding not only doctrine but also matters pertaining to morality and social justice. The Catholic view is based on the primacy of Peter and the belief that the Holy Spirit directly intervenes to guard the Church from error.

In the area of prayer and the theology of redemption, Protestant theology has tended to deal with the human situation first and then with the theological aspect of the issue. In other words, Protestant spirituality, generally, begins at the point of human need, because of original sin, thus pinpointing the need for redemption and Christ,[69] whereas Catholic theology tends to emphasize more that God created us out of love, and that human nature is basically good. It is because of this love that we were redeemed, not because of our sin. (The reader wishing to pursue similar lines of thought further may refer to the writings of Bernard Lonergan and Matthew Fox and also sources on Franciscan spirituality.) In addition, Protestant theology has been, traditionally, more open to secular sources of human learning and growth than the Catholic viewpoint, believing that these, too, can be instruments of the Holy Spirit.[70]

Regarding the mode of prayer itself, until the charismatic renewal, Catholics have traditionally favored using formal prayer, as compared to the Protestant emphasis of more informal and spontaneous personal prayer. Thus, in the context of worship, the Protestant emphasis has been upon reading and preaching the word and upon spontaneous personal prayer. The Catholic tradition includes reading the Scriptures, but there is less emphasis upon good preaching and opportunity for spontaneous shared prayer. The formal ritual of the sacrament of the Eucharist, or the Lord's supper, has been emphasized as the highlight of worship.

If we look at the spiritual journey itself, Protestant traditions have also tended to emphasize the initial aspects of conversion, as opposed to discipling or nurturing the growing Christian. The latter has been more the orientation of the Catholic Church through asceticism, the sacraments, liturgy, and spiritual direction. However, it has been pointed out that, in many cases, Catholic asceticism has lost sight of the Gospel,[71] and that Protestant worship and spirituality has been greatly impoverished by the lack of liturgical practice and spiritual direction available to growing Christians.[72]

Finally, it can be said that with the exception of Pentecostals and Quakers, both Catholics and Protestant Christians had lost a sense of awareness of the central role of the Holy Spirit in Christian spirituality.[73] In the last two decades, the charismatic renewal has revolutionized segments of Protestant and Catholic spirituality. Through the charismatic renewal, Catholics have become more free and spontaneous in their prayer expressions. They have experienced a deep need for making the Scriptures a living part of their faith. They have also become more keenly aware of the need for a conscious and explicit commitment of faith in Christ for a mature spirituality. Similarly, a large number of Protestants, of all denominations, have experienced a greater need for the reception of the sacrament of the Lord's supper. They have also grown in their appreciation of the liturgical aspects of worship and of spiritual direction. We can say that in many cases the effect of the renewal has been a greater sense of balance and complementarity among both Catholics and Protestants, as well as a greater appreciation of each other's traditions.

For our purposes here, if we take an overall look at these traditions, I believe it is legitimate to say that Catholic spirituality, more so than its Protestant counterpart, generally has placed more of an emphasis on the feminine mode of being in its receptive approach to prayer, its emphasis on the theology of redemption, liturgical aspects of worship and the nurture and growth of the individual Christian. The Protestant traditions, with some definite exceptions, have tended to be more active in their spiritual pursuits, that is, more focused on what humans can do, for example, in regard to study of the Scriptures, evangelism, and social justice.

The ultimate objective of this work is to present a balanced approach of Christian spirituality which gives due attention to the feminine mode. The next chapter concerns itself with such a program.

Notes

1. Evelyn Underhill, *Practical Mysticism* (New York: E.P. Dutton and Co., 1943), p. 27.

2. *Idem, Mystics of the Church* (Cambridge: James Clarke and Co., 1975), pp. 14–15.

3. *Idem, Practical Mysticism*, p. 116.

4. *Idem, Mystics of the Church*, p. 20.

5. *Ibid.*, pp. 26–28.

6. St. Teresa of Avila, *Interior Castle*, trans. E.A. Peers (New York: Image Books, Doubleday and Co., 1961), p. 8.

7. Jordan Aumann, O.P., *Teresa's Interior Castle*, Tape No. 1 (Notre Dame: Ave Maria Press, 1978).

8. *Ibid.*, Tape No. 2.

9. *Ibid.*

10. Evelyn Underhill, *Mystics of the Church*, p. 180.

11. Georgia Harkness, *Mysticism* (New York: Abingdon Press, 1973), p. 126.

12. St. Ignatius of Loyola, *The Spiritual Exercises*, trans. A. Mottola (New York: Image Books, Doubleday and Co., 1964), p. 14.

13. John English, S.J., *Spiritual Freedom* (Guelph: Loyola House, 1974), pp. 98–99.

14. *Ibid.*, p. 180.

15. *Ibid.*, pp. 100–101.

16. *Ibid.*, p. 108.

17. St. Ignatius of Loyola, *The Spiritual Exercises*, pp. 14–15.

18. John English, S.J., *Spiritual Freedom*, pp. 195–197.

19. *Ibid.*, p. 227.

20. St. Ignatius of Loyola, *The Spiritual Exercises*, p. 15.

21. *Ibid.*

22. John English, S.J., *Spiritual Freedom*, p. 250.

23. Evelyn Underhill, *Practical Mysticism*, p. xi.

24. *Ibid.*, p. 29.

25. *Ibid.*, pp. 44–45.

26. *Ibid.*, p. 46.

27. *Ibid.*, p. 48.

28. *Ibid.*, p. 51.

29. *Ibid.*, pp. 54–55.

30. *Ibid.*, p. 56.

31. *Ibid.*, p. 57.

32. *Ibid.*, pp. 90–91.

33. *Ibid.*, pp. 97–99.

34. *Ibid.,* p. 119.

35. *Ibid.,* pp. 127–129.

36. *Ibid.,* p. 47.

37. *Idem, The Spiritual Life* (New York: Harper and Row, n.d.), p. 91.

38. *Ibid.,* p. 36.

39. *Ibid.,* p. 37.

40. Thomas Merton, *Life and Holiness* (New York: Image Books, Doubleday and Co., 1964), p. 29.

41. *Ibid.,* p. 54.

42. *Ibid.,* p. 24.

43. *Ibid.,* p. 25.

44. *Ibid.,* p. 37.

45. *Ibid.,* p. 25.

46. *Ibid.,* p. 30.

47. *Ibid.,* p. 67.

48. *Ibid.,* p. 78.

49. *Idem, New Seeds of Contemplation* (New York: New Directions Co., 1972), p. 225.

50. *Ibid.,* p. 126.

51. *Idem, Life and Holiness,* pp. 34–36.

52. *Idem, New Seeds of Contemplation,* pp. 74–75.

53. *Ibid.,* p. 224.

54. *Ibid.,* p. 214.

55. *Ibid.,* p. 217.

56. *Ibid.,* pp. 215–216.

57. *Ibid.,* p. 230.

58. *Ibid.,* p. 208.

59. *Ibid.,* pp. 207–208.

60. *Ibid.,* p. 235.

61. *Ibid.,* p. 21.

62. *Ibid.,* p. 53.

63. *Ibid.,* p. 108.

64. *Ibid.,* p. 267.

65. *Ibid.,* pp. 194–196.

66. *Ibid.,* p. 192.

67. Douglas Steere, "Common Frontiers in Catholic and Non-Catholic Spirituality," *Protestants and Catholics on the*

Spiritual Life, ed. Michael Mark, O.S.B. (Collegeville: The Liturgical Press, 1965), p. 42.

68. *Ibid.,* p. 45.

69. John B. Coburn, "Contemporary Non-Catholic Spirituality and the Guidance of Souls," *Protestants and Catholics on the Spiritual Life,* p. 57.

70. *Ibid.,* pp. 59–60.

71. Bernard Häring, C.SS.R., "A Modern Approach to the Ascetical Life," *Protestants and Catholics on the Spiritual Life,* p. 82.

72. Douglas Steere, "Common Frontiers in Catholic and Non-Catholic Spirituality," *Protestants and Catholics on the Spiritual Life,* p. 51.

73. Kilian McDonnell, O.S.B., "Problems and Perspectives: An Epilogue," *Protestants and Catholics on the Spiritual Life,* pp. 97–98.

5

The Covenant Life: Seven Dimensions of Christian Spirituality

Introduction

The Covenant Life Program is the result of three years of academic research and personal and professional experience. It grew out of my own spiritual search and interest in the psychology of Carl Jung. I chose Jung because he provides the best psychological vantage point for the understanding of the spiritual life.

The program attempts to provide a wholistic experience for Christian spiritual development. It begins with the individual's search for meaning and purpose in life and moves through the integration of all aspects of faith nurture and experience, resulting in a life of ministry through the Holy Spirit. Each of the spiritual dimensions could be developed into its own book by itself. Yet, this program provides for a depth experience, within the format of each element of spiritual growth identified. It leads the person to make a personal connection from his/her life story at each stage, and it invites open and non-judgmental reflection. These are the seeds of creativity and learning and akin to the Jungian concept of the feminine mode.

The program involves four formal presentations, referred to as theoretical Foundations, and nine work sessions, each composed of (a) Scripture, (b) Perspective, (c) Exercise, (d) Closing Meditation, and (e) For Further Reading.

The overall program entails approximately ten to sixteen hours. It can be experienced by a group or done individually (either on a weekly basis for seven to eight weeks, or in a weekend context, etc.). It begins with a section of the Search for Meaning, which is a natural part of the middle years of adulthood, followed by a session of Adult Development, from a Jungian perspective. Then, the seven dimensions of Christian spiritual growth are presented as follows: (1) Conversion—The Turning Point, (2) The Covenant Relationship in the Bible, (3) Prayer and Presence, (4) Mature Love and Relationships, (5) Reconciliation—Confession and Inner Healing, (6) Celebration and Community, and (7) A Living Ministry—The Fruit of the Holy Spirit.

Guided meditation and journal writing were chosen as the modes for the personal exercises because they encourage the expression of the feminine mode in the human personality. The latter, as stated in this work earlier, is essential for the development of the life of the Spirit. There are other modes of expression, such as art work and poetry, which are compatible with the feminine mode. Program participants may be encouraged to express themselves in a variety of ways, especially if journal writing is particularly difficult for some.

To some, it may seem that the program attempts too much in too little time. However, there is such a need for a wholistic foundation for the Christian faith that I opted to take the risk. In some cases, what we have available in our Christian churches is very one-sided. We neglect to integrate concepts from other denominations with a different emphasis, resulting in a spirituality that is out of balance or stunted in its growth. The latter is what we present to the world. It is no wonder the institutional churches are declining in membership.

Participants are encouraged to be open and honest in their journal writing and in sharing with others. The latter is optional to insure spontaneity and truthfulness. Individuals are also encouraged to be open to new ways of learning and to new ideas, even regarding issues which they have considered before. Dreams should be especially noted and recorded in the journal, as they are a unique expression of the unconscious and of our life situations.

Learning is directly proportionate to receptivity. Therefore, maintaining an attitude of openness insures us of maximum benefit and gain from this program. God can only come into our lives to the extent that we allow him to do so. Making a conscious decision to be open to his Spirit is an important first step before embarking on this growth journey.

The group should maintain a supportive attitude as well as respect the needs of individuals for quiet time and separateness. It is best if the program takes place in a home-type of setting, as opposed to a classroom or conference room. There should be comfortable seats and a relaxed atmosphere. The leader or facilitator's primary role is listening to the needs that emerge, affirming and encouraging individuals to explore avenues of growth, and protecting individuals and the group as a whole from disruption of the supportive atmosphere and process. Individuals should assume responsbility for being on time for the sessions and for their own learning experience overall.

The Foundation sections can be read by individuals before coming to the program sessions or included in the program as formal teaching presentations. An outline of each is provided in order to review the material for participants or as a guide for the leader presenting it. Participants are encouraged to listen more than to take notes during these, as well as during the Perspective sessions. While Scriptures are read at the beginning and end of the work sessions, you are encouraged to sit in a comfortable position, be still and listen to God's word, as if he is speaking directly to you and your specific life situation. Maintain a meditative posture, allowing feelings and/or images to emerge freely as they will.

In journal writing, participants are asked to avoid being concerned with writing complete sentences, or worrying about spelling, or punctuation, or how it all sounds. Instead, they are encouraged to allow themselves to write freely and spontaneously, without censure or judgment, trusting the Spirit of God to touch their own spirits within. At the end of the Exercises the option to share with another is suggested. If the program is conducted with a group, participants may break up into pairs and share with their partners the most significant learning they experienced. Individuals may be encouraged by the leader to pray for partners in a special way for the duration of the program. In going through the program individually, a person may choose to share significant learnings with a close friend and ask the latter to pray for him/her as he/she goes through the experience.

In the sections For Further Reading, certain references have an asterisk indicating those which are most closely related to the topic. If the program is conducted on a weekly basis, participants can be encouraged to read one of the books listed as preparation for each session.

My hope is that the Covenant Life Program will revitalize the faith of those who are already committed Christians and move those who are only seekers to thirst for more.

Appendices C and D, at the end of this work, include evaluation forms which may be used at the beginning and at the end of the program, when it is offered in a group setting.

THE SEARCH FOR MEANING—
A SEARCH FOR GOD

Scriptures:

. . . you will seek the Lord your God, and you will find him, if you search for him with all your heart, and with all your soul.

(Dt 4:29)

Ask and it will be given you; seek and you will find; knock and it will be opened to you. For everyone who asks receives, and he who seeks finds, and to him who knocks it will be opened.

(Mt 7:7–8)

Foundations:

A. The Problem—Lack of Meaning
   (1) We do not take time to listen to our inner selves.
   (2) Lack of meaning is a universal experience; it may be manifested in several ways:
      (a) reaching the middle years;
      (b) experiencing a death or terminal illness of someone close or ourselves;
      (c) experiencing boredom, apathy or feeling insignificant in a complex world.
   (3) We tend to search for meaning, first, outside of ourselves.
   (4) The emptiness or lack of meaning can be an opportunity for growth.
   (5) Quiet and solitude nurture this growth.
   (6) We fear solitude because we associate it with loneliness.

B. Obstacles to the Discovery of Meaning
   (1) In the nineteenth century the "self" replaces the "soul."
   (2) Maslow resolves the dichotomy between objective and subjective experiences.
   (3) In the past, we overlooked the function of the left and right brain hemispheres.
   (4) We have emphasized left brain functions in our Western educational systems.

C. Where Meaning Is Found
   (1) Meaning takes place in our personal life stories.
   (2) There are three basic movements of the human life story.
   (3) Maslow points out characteristics of self-actualizing people.

(4) The answer lies beyond self-actualization, i.e., in self-transcendence.

(5) The non-rational aspects of faith relate to the feminine mode.

(6) C.G. Jung believes that in the deepest part of the psyche lies a divine imprint.

(7) There are three aspects of the ultimate search for meaning.

(8) The Christian contexts for the engagement with God, self and others are:

    (a) Scriptures;
    (b) prayer;
    (c) worship and sacraments;
    (d) mature relationships with others.

(9) Where we Christians have failed.

Perspective:

Each event that we experience in our life journey is not isolated as an event or a relationship or an experience. It is a part of our unique life story, which itself is a part of the life story of the universe. The meaning to be found in each event reveals itself much in the same manner that we begin to see the total picture of a large puzzle after we have many pieces together, or much in the same way that a sculpture or a painting or another creative project begins to take shape and finally resemble the finished product we hoped for. If we focused merely on each part, or stage, outside of the total work, its significance would be severely limited. As an individual and as a therapist, I know that looking at life in this context is one of the best antidotes to depression, despair and alienation, because it views each event as part of a meaningful whole. Approach the following exercise from this perspective.

Exercise:

(1) Sit in a comfortable chair, making sure that your body is in a comfortable position. Close your eyes

and take four or five very deep breaths, counting them slowly. Focus your attention on relaxing every muscle and part of your body; then resume your normal breathing rate in a relaxed manner.

(2)   Let your mind wander a bit throughout your entire life story and recall, in a relaxed fashion, those specific events or experiences which have helped you, in a special way, to enlarge the meaning and purpose of your existence. Do not focus on any one in detail; simply let each one present itself before you and acknowledge them briefly, one by one.

(3)   Open your eyes and list as many of these events and experiences as you can remember, briefly, with only a phrase or two, or with a sentence, just enough for you to be able to identify each and recall it later.

(4)   After you have completed your list, choose one of these instances to focus on, and write several paragraphs merely describing the experience itself and how it was helpful to you, without judging it or interpreting it in any way. Tell it as if you were telling the story to someone else.

(5)   After you are finished writing, read what you have written to yourself; then close your eyes and be aware of your feelings about what you just read. Note whatever spontaneous impressions or images may come to your mind and heart. Do not force any of these things; merely let them happen, and make note of them in your notebook.

(6)   Afterward, if you wish, share what you have written with another person, not necessarily for the purpose of getting feedback or judgment, but just to share it.

Closing Meditation:

For thus says the Lord God: Behold, I, I myself will search for my sheep, and will seek them out. As a shep-

herd seeks out his flock when some of his sheep have
been scattered abroad, so I will seek out my sheep; and I
will rescue them. . . . And I will bring them out . . . and
gather them . . . and I will feed them. . . . I myself will be
the shepherd of my sheep. . . . I will seek the lost, and I
will bring back the strayed, and I will bind up the crip-
pled, and I will strengthen the weak, and the fat and
strong I will watch over; I will feed them in justice

(Ez 34:11–16).

For Further Reading:

*"The Book of Ecclesiastes," *The Bible*
Time & Myth, John Dunne
Man's Search for Meaning, Viktor Frankl
To a Dancing God, Sam Keen
If You Meet the Buddah on the Road, Kill Him! Shel-
    don Kopp
Gifts From the Sea, Anne Morrow Lindberg
Journey Inward, Journey Outward, Elizabeth O'Connor
The Psychology of Consciousness, Robert Ornstein
The Meaning of Persons, Paul Tournier

ADULT PSYCHOLOGICAL DEVELOPMENT
AND THE RECEPTIVE MODE

Scriptures:

Now the word of the Lord came to me saying: Before I
formed you in the womb I knew you and before you
were born I consecrated you

(Jer 1:4–5).

The Lord called me from the womb, from the body of
my mother he named my name

(Is (49:1).

Foundations:

A. The Human Life Stages
   (1) Psychological research is available on adult development.
   (2) Jung provides an outline of human development and a focus for the second half of our lifetimes.

B. The Inner Search
   (1) Lack of meaning prompts us to ask a question about our personal identity, which answer can only come from *within* ourselves.
   (2) We realize ourselves through our choice of vocation, which includes a spirtuality.

C. Neurosis and the Absence of Meaning
   (1) Many people who come to counseling are experiencing a lack of meaning.
   (2) Neurosis can point to a new possibility of growth.

D. The Inner Search and Religious Experience
   (1) The basis of faith is spontaneous religious experience.
   (2) Religion is one of the earliest of most universal activities of the human mind.
   (3) Jung's perspective regarding chance is that it is a symptom of an alienated life.

E. The Emergence of a Religious Life
   (1) Religious experiences have the power to turn us around.
   (2) God is more than our image of God.
   (3) Many so-called Christians have failed to consider a personal encounter with Christ.

(4) There is a parallel between ego development and the development of the spiritual life.
(5) The process of becoming empty and the feminine aspect of the human personality are analogous.
(6) Spiritual rebirth is an ancient concept.

F. The Significance of the Symbolic
(1) God is inexpressible in human language.
(2) The excessive use of reason creates a problem.
(3) Symbolism and imagination are means for expressing life's mysteries.
(4) Symbols help us to make connections.

G. The Feminine as a Modality of Being
(1) Review feminine values in history.
(2) In the sight of God, the masculine and the feminine are complementary.
(3) There are several approaches to the feminine and Jung's contribution is unique.

H. Characteristics of the Feminine (The Receptive Mode)
(1) The feminine mode is more than sexual identity; it also includes:

    (a) styles of awareness;
    (b) ways of relating;
    (c) ways of internalizing reality;
    (d) modes of making judgments and decisions.

(2) Intuition and knowing can be expressed in the context of the feminine mode.
(3) Jung's anima and animus are conceptual aids.
(4) The feminine and masculine functions are complementary.

      (5)   The feminine and masculine modes can have both positive and negative functions.

I.   Spirituality and the Feminine
      (1)   Jung believed that women are naturally more receptive to the Spirit of God.
      (2)   There are several stages of development of the feminine mode.
      (3)   There is a relationship between the feminine mode and mature love.
      (4)   Meditative prayer relates to the feminine mode.
      (5)   Christian spirituality is always in the context of relationship.
      (6)   For the integrated person there is no dichotomy between body and spirit, or religion and life.
      (7)   The experience of God is always individual and personal, e.g., Jesus' means of communication was in a feminine context—through parable, symbol and living example.
      (8)   Summarize the overall activity of the feminine mode.

Perspective:

In the first session of the Covenant Life Program we focused on one significant event which enlarged one's life purpose and meaning. In this session we want to look at the life journey as a whole, particularly focusing on the spiritual search. The perspective which will facilitate our task here is that of the mode of consciousness which we will refer to as a "creative receptivity." We will not use the words feminine, passive, etc., because most of us have too many negative stereotypes regarding these, and neither is completely true to the meaning we wish to convey. This mode of consciousness is referred to as a "creative receptivity" because it conveys both a movement inward as well as an outward creative expression.

The difference between the two modes of consciousness can be exemplified in terms of the way a botanist vs. a poet know and experience a flower. A botanist knows it by studying each part of its roots, stem, leaves and each of its flower parts, classifying them by shape, size and color. A poet can see the same flower and know it by letting its beauty become a part of himself. Both kinds of knowledge are just as real. In experiencing God, reason and words will take us only so far. At this point, we need to let go of reason to some extent, and rely more on the poet's wordless kind of knowledge, such as intuition, imagery, symbols and insights.

In our Western culture symbols are not talked about a great deal. A word should be said here about the difference between a sign and a symbol, before going on to the practical exercise of this section. A sign's meaning is usually rather explicit, discrete and identifiable. It stands for something very specific, e.g., a stop sign on a street corner. A symbol points to a meaning which is deeper, and which cannot be completely grasped or boxed-in, e.g., the symbol of a cross can mean that a person is a Christian; that he/she is one with other Christian believers; it also stands for Christ and his life, death and resurrection; it can convey a meaning related to the time when a person acquired it, i.e., there could be a special experience or event related to it, like the end of a retreat, etc. There is no way to exhaust all the possible implications of such a powerful symbol. Also, a sign, in some cases, can be a symbol, e.g., in a person's dream there may be a stop sign that appears at a crossroads. In this case, the individual's unconscious has chosen a simple sign, which is part of the everyday experience of the person, to symbolize a significant message about that person's life, e.g., maybe the individual has been drinking heavily and his/her psyche, in its wisdom, is saying "Stop! There may be danger ahead!"

Exercise:

(1)   Now get your body in a relaxed and comfortable position and proceed with the breathing exercise as you did in the last session.

(2)   With your eyes closed and your body relaxed, get a sense of your own unique spiritual search, from its very beginning, i.e., from your birth onward. Let your mind and heart reveal to you the stages of the journey, each with its own unique circumstances, persons and events. Do not focus at length on any one stage; simply view them as if they were on a screen before you.

(3)   Open your eyes and write down the life stages of your spiritual autobiography, beginning at the time you were born up to the present. Write down a phrase or two, or a sentence, for each. Describe your experience to date in about eight to twelve stages.

(4)   When you finish writing these, read them only to yourself; then close your eyes and be sensitive to the feelings and impressions that come from within you. As you experience these write them down in your notebook, without much elaboration or interpretation. Simply record them.

(5)   Choose one of the stages which you have written down (only not the most recent) and elaborate upon it, writing down in more detail what kind of a time it was for you, including the persons and events and feelings that were significant within that stage, as well as any other factors which came to your mind at this time.

(6)   When you have finished elaborating upon it, read slowly what you have written; then choose a symbol from your experience which you feel would be representative of this stage.

(7)   After you identify a symbol, write about its relationship to that stage, and describe why you felt it was appropriate. You may wish to express your symbol through another art form, such as drawing or poetry.

(8)   If you wish to do so, share any part of the whole of your writing and reflection with someone else.

Closing Meditation:

For everything there is a season
 and a time for every matter under heaven:
A time to be born, and a time to die;
 a time to plant, and a time to pluck up what is
 planted;
A time to kill, and a time to heal;
 a time to break down, and a time to build up;
A time to weep, and a time to laugh;
 a time to mourn, and a time to dance;
A time to cast away stones, and a time to gather stones
 together;
 a time to embrace, and a time to refrain from
 embracing;
A time to seek, and a time to lose;
 a time to keep, and a time to cast away;
A time to rend, and a time to sew;
 a time to keep silence, and a time to speak;
A time to love, and a time to hate;
 a time for war, and a time for peace.

What gain has the worker from his toil? . . . it is
God's gift to man that everyone should . . . take pleasure
in all his toil. I know that whatever God does endures
forever; nothing can be added to it, nor anything taken
from it

(Eccl 3:1–9. 13–14).

For Further Reading:

*"The Book of Exodus," *The Bible*
Journey to Self, Tom Downs
Telling Your Story, Sam Keen and Anne Fox
The Taste of New Wine, Keith Miller
Ascent of the Mountain and Flight of the Dove,
 Michael Novak
**Passages,* Gail Sheehy

ELEMENTS OF CONTEMPORARY CHRISTIAN SPIRITUALITY

This section of the Covenant Life Program corresponds to Chapter 3 of this work, and it contains the theoretical foundations for the remaining sections of this program. The leader may choose to present it as a whole and then proceed with the perspective and exercises sections corresponding to each of the dimensions identified.

Foundations:

A. Introduction
    (1) God is the ultimate object of our search for meaning and wholeness (Ch. 1).
    (2) The feminine, as a modality of being, is an essential factor in the spiritual growth journey (Ch. 2).

B. Spirituality Resists Definition
    (1) There is a lack of understanding about the term spirituality.
    (2) There are several important aspects of Christian spirituality as a whole:

        (a) a way of life, lifelong and transformative;
        (b) the realization of the human personality according to God's plan for each of us;
        (c) the supportive discipline which makes possible the growth and practice of our faith;
        (d) the living out of the Spirit of Jesus within each of us.

    (3) Christian spirituality entails:

        (a) a personal knowledge of Jesus, the Father and the Spirit;

(b) a mature understanding of the human personality;
(c) the practice of prayer;
(d) the experience of mature love;
(e) the awareness of the nature of evil;
(f) participation in the celebration of our faith in the context of the Christian community;
(g) furthering the kingdom in ministry to others through the Holy Spirit.

C. Conscious Choice—Rebirth
(1) The beginning of the Christian spiritual journey requires a conscious choice and commitment.
(2) This conscious choice must be an individual act; we must do it alone.
(3) The nature of the choice and commitment has to do with taking a stand about our ultimate life values. For the Christian it ultimately has to do with the identity of Jesus of Nazareth.
(4) Meditation on the Scriptures is the most direct means for growing in the knowledge of Jesus.

D. Creative Solitude—The Womb
(1) We need to unhook from the activity of modern living to make time and space for solitude.
(2) We need to make the transition from loneliness to solitude.
(3) Silence and solitude offer us a creative and fresh outlook on life.
(4) The key is *balance* between silence and words, withdrawal and involvement, distance and closeness, and solitude and community.

(5) There is a difference in silence and detachment in the East vs. the West.

E. The Gift of Prayer—The Child
  (1) Prayer is the fruit of the reborn self.
  (2) It is the way in which the deepest part of us touches God and we are touched by him.
  (3) We cannot pray by ourselves; God's Spirit prays in us.
  (4) When we get depressed in our spiritual life, we forget that prayer is a gift (grace).
  (5) Prayer must be a priority for the Christian.
  (6) Prayer is more than conversation with God.
  (7) In contemplative prayer we focus our attention completely upon God, not upon our needs or requests.

F. Love and Relationships
  (1) God is interested in the physical world— Jesus became a man.
  (2) Love and compassion are an integral part of Christian spirituality. Compassion means to enter into the suffering of another with passion.
  (3) The ultimate goal of prayer is love.
  (4) Love and relationships are the way in which we live out our Christian spirituality.

G. Dreams—Inner Wisdom
  (1) Dreams are primary points of contact with the unconscious.
  (2) Dreams are a means of revelation about the underlying meaning of life and therefore of God.
  (3) The function of dreams is one of reconciling ourselves to our deepest center and, therefore, to God's purpose within us.

(4) Our dreams are reproductions of our inner life situations.

H. Encounter with Darkness
   (1) There are three manifestations of the phenomenon of evil:

   (a) the evil in ourselves;
   (b) the role of suffering;
   (c) evil as a separate spiritual entity.

   (2) The shadow is the inferior, unwanted part of our personality.
   (3) There is a transformative aspect of suffering.
   (4) Evil works for dissociation, disintegration and separation from God.

I. Celebration and Community
   (1) The church is the ultimate and corporate expression of the kingdom of God on earth.
   (2) The Scriptures indicate that to be mature Christians we need to relate to a faith community.
   (3) The Christian community nurtures and feeds our faith, through the sacraments and worship.
   (4) The sacraments serve as concrete focal points of God's caring presence with us.
   (5) The sacrament of baptism celebrates the individual's rebirth and entry into the Christian community.
   (6) The sacrament of the Lord's supper is Christ's gift of self which transforms us even in our present life circumstances.
   (7) The importance of the sacraments is to affirm us, to connect us with history and to provide us with hope and expectation.
   (8) The physical nature of the sacraments is an important reminder of the incarnation.

    (9)   The community protects and affirms our prayer life.

  (10)   Obedience means responsive listening and accountability.

FIRST DIMENSION:
"CONVERSION—THE TURNING POINT"

Scriptures:

For God so loved the world that he gave his one and only Son, that whosoever believes in him shall not perish, but have eternal life. For God did not send his Son into the world to condemn the world, but to save the world through him

(Jn 3:16–17).

Jesus said, "I am the way and the truth and the life. No one comes to the Father except through me"

(Jn 14:6).

Whoever acknowledges me before men, I will also acknowledge him before my Father in heaven, but whoever denies me before men, I will also deny him before my Father

(Mt 10:32).

Perspective:

Conversion is the first stepping stone of the Christian journey. It is the point at which the individual confronts, face-to-face, the "bottom line" questions of life, having to do with the origin and meaning of life and the universe, the existence of God, death, etc., and makes a conscious commitment to his/her faith values.

Sid Simon, the humanistic educator, tells us that before

something can be a full value, it must first meet certain criteria. It must be:

(1) *chosen freely,* from among alternatives, after being given due reflection;
(2) prized, cherished, and *publicly affirmed;*
(3) *acted upon* and part of a pattern that is a repeated action.[1]

This is true of all values, and it is especially true of the ultimate life values of which we speak. A value that meets the above criteria is obviously one which must also be a conscious choice.

The word conversion, used to connote this rebirth experience, implies a change (from the Greek, to revert, to turn). A change will always occur when we assume a new value in our life experience, because, as pointed out above, a true value is one which will be integrated into our behavior pattern on a regular basis. When we talk about spiritual rebirth or conversion, all we are talking about is making a conscious choice to integrate certain values, about the ultimate meaning of life, into our own life experiences.

Many individuals automatically and blindly reject Christianity, because they understand making a Christain faith commitment, primarily, as a requirement to make major changes in their lives. This is an erroneous outlook and truly a misunderstanding of the priorities of the Christian faith.

In any kind of rebirth or conversion (Christian or not): (1) something has *led* the individual to *seek* new meaning and purpose; (2) he/she at some point *experiences a new awareness or value* about the meaning of life; (3) he/she finally *makes a conscious decision* to adopt the new understanding or value into his/her own life experience. In this section we will focus upon the first two aspects of the rebirth experience. The section on covenant will deal with the third.

The unique aspects of a Christian conversion in particular are that:

(1) the Christian views the desire to seek a deeper life meaning itself as *God-initiated* (the leading of the Holy

Spirit) since he/she understands human life as being God's creation;

(2)   the individual sees the choice to respond and relate to God as a *free choice,* since Christian theology assumes that humans have a free will;

(3)   the choice made has to do with a *relationship,* primarily the relationship of the person with God as he manifested himself in Jesus, his Son, whose Spirit dwells in the heart of the Christian.

I will say more about these aspects of the Christian faith in the second dimension of this work "The Covenant Relationship in the Bible." The point I am making here, however, is that the choice has to do with a relationship primarily (thus the title word covenant) and not with a series of rules for behavior or dogmas. We arrive at individual guidelines for behavior later, as we discern our unique and personal relationship with God, and not the other way around.

Exercise:

(1)   Sit in a comfortable position, as you have done before, focusing on the rhythm of your breathing and concentrating on relaxing, and nothing more.

(2)   With your eyes closed, listen to your inner self; ask yourself the questions: "What do I really believe about life? What values are really important to me? What do I really believe about God?"

(3)   Be honest with yourself; disregard for now what you think you should say or what you were taught from parents, teachers, or the church. Simply listen to the impressions that come from your own inner self, and write about them in your notebook.

(4)   Are the values you identified consistent with your behavior and how you spend your time? What conflicts are you experiencing? What issues need to be reconciled?

(5)   If you were completely free to design your life situ-

ation, what would it look like? When you feel ready, write about it in your notebook without censuring or judging your statements.

(6)   When you finish writing, reread what you have written, slowly, and then close your eyes and give yourself an opportunity to perceive your feelings, impressions, and images about what you have written. Record whatever elements of your experience you wish.

(7)   If you like, share what you have written with another person.

Closing Meditation:

Jesus began to teach. . . . He taught them many things by parables and (he) said: "Listen! A farmer went out to sow his seed. As he was scattering his seed, some fell among the path, and the birds came and ate it up. Some fell on rocky places, where it did not have much soil. It sprang up quickly, because the soil was shallow. But when the sun came up, the plants were scorched, and they withered because they had no root. Other seed fell among thorns, which grew up and choked the plants, so that they did not bear grain. Still other seed fell on good ground. It came up, grew and produced a crop, multiplying thirty, sixty, or even a hundred times." Then Jesus said, "He who has ears to hear, let him hear."

Then Jesus said to them . . . "The farmer sows the word. Some people are like the seed along the path, where the word is sown. As soon as they hear it, Satan comes and takes away the word that was sown in them. Others are like the seed sown in rocky places; they hear the word and at once receive it with joy. But since they have no root, they last only a short time. When trouble or persecution comes because of the word, they quickly fall away. Still others, like seed sown among thorns, hear the word; but the worries of this life, the deceitfulness of wealth and the desires for other things come in and choke the word, making it unfruitful. Others, like seed sown on good soil, hear the word, accept it, and produce a crop thirty, sixty, or even a hundred times that which was sown"

(Mk 4:1–9. 13–20).

For Further Reading:

*"The Book of Genesis," *The Bible*
Man the Choice Maker, Howes and Moon
Encounter with God, Morton Kelsey
Myth, History and Faith, Morton Kelsey
Mere Christianity, C.S. Lewis
More Than a Carpenter, Josh McDowell
The Return to Faith, Clyde Reid
Meeting Yourself Halfway, Sidney Simon

SECOND DIMENSION:
"THE COVENANT RELATIONSHIP IN THE BIBLE"

Scriptures:

Man shall not live by bread alone, but by every word that proceeds from the mouth of God

(Mt 4:4).

This book . . . shall not depart out of your mouth but you shall meditate on it day and night . . . for then you shall make your way prosperous and then you shall have good success

(Jos 1:8).

> Faith comes from hearing the message, and the message is heard through the word of Christ
>
> (Rom 10:17).

> If you confess with your mouth "Jesus is Lord" and believe in your heart that God raised him from the dead, you will be saved. For it is with your heart that you believe and are justified, and it is with your mouth that you confess and are saved
>
> (Rom 10:9).

Perspective:

The Scriptures are the backbone of Christian spirituality. They are the primary instrument without which it is impossible to navigate. The Scriptures are significant for the development of a spiritual life for two reasons: first, they tell the history of God's revelation of himself, his relationship to humankind and his overall purpose for the world which he created; second, they provide us with concrete guidelines for the maturation and growth of our faith regarding (a) our growing knowledge of the person of Christ, the Father, and the Holy Spirit, (b) the practice of prayer, (c) our relationships with others, and (d) discerning God's will for our lives.

In this section the focus will be primarily on the importance of the Scriptures regarding God's revelation of himself in his relationship to humankind and the world which he created. Other sections of this work will deal with the remaining aspects mentioned above. The overall story of salvation for humankind is found in the Scriptures as the history of God's revelation of himself to the Israelites.

The primary theme in the Scriptures is that of relationship in the context of love. Everything that we find in the Old and New Testaments (covenants) must be evaluated and understood in this context, in order to remain true to the overall meaning and purpose of the Bible.

It was out of love and in love that God created humankind and the universe. In his own likeness God gave human beings a

creative intelligence and the capability to love, both of which include and necessitate a free will; for there is no such thing as love
or creativity without freedom of choice. Consistent with love, the
nature of God's creation was and is good. The first chapter of
Genesis states it no less than six times.

In his desire for a love relationship with his creation, the Father established a covenant (i.e., guidelines to protect the relationship), which human beings were free to accept or reject. Our
early ancestors (Adam and Eve and the first generations of humanity) chose to break the covenant, and they suffered because
of their choice to isolate themselves from the Father (which is the
nature of sin). But God, in his everlasting love, faithfulness and
creativity, re-established the covenant through one whom he
found to be responsive and faithful, i.e., Abram.

Through Abraham and his descendants (the Israelites), the
Father re-established the covenant. He gradually revealed more
and more of himself to his people, and promised them ultimate
fulfillment as a result of their obedience (from the Latin, responsive listening) to the covenant. He brought them out of the bondage of slavery in Egypt, and into the promised land. We find that
during and after the journey, human response varied, and at
times faithfulness to the covenant on the part of the Israelites
faded altogether. Time and time again the people fell away from
the covenant and sought fulfillment away from the Father, as
they did before. As a result, after a period of greatness and pros-
perity, Israel was divided and taken captive again. Later, a rem-
nant of the captive nation returned to their own land to attempt
to re-establish their national life and heritage.

The Father's love and fidelity, however, was unchanging and
everlasting, and he promised an even more creative means for the
restoration of the covenant through one who was like us, a human being who was also his Son. The Father's desire and hope
was that, through this explicit and human manifestation of his
love for us, which is Christ, humans would choose to know him
and experience the ultimate and complete fulfillment, available
in relationship with him, our Creator and Father.

This is the covenant story in the Bible. Nothing in the Scriptures makes any sense if it is viewed outside of this context.

Christians can become discouraged and neurotic and can severely misinterpret Christianity to others when they view any event or section of the Scriptures outside of this context.

The Christian faith makes absolutely no sense outside of the context of a relationship of love. When Christ was asked which was the greatest commandment, he did not mention any specific sin such as adultery, divorce, homosexuality, keeping the Sabbath, fasting, almsgiving, etc. Instead he said:

> Love the Lord your God with all your heart, with all your soul, and with all your mind. This is the first and greatest commandment.

And he quickly added:

> And the second is like it: Love your neighbor as yourself. All the law and the prophets hang on these two commandments (Mt 22:37–40).

Christ undoubtedly shocked many of his contemporaries. When God promised the Israelites a Savior, they assumed that it would be a mighty and powerful king or political leader, with all the pomp and regalia that is customary regarding such powerful figures. But in the Book of the prophet Isaiah God says:

> For my thoughts are not your thoughts,
>   neither are your ways my ways, says the Lord.
> For as the heavens are higher than the earth,
>   so are my ways higher than your ways
>   and my thoughts than your thoughts (Is 55:8–9).

Instead, the Father sent his Son, a carpenter, who led a quiet existence for the first thirty years of his life and who, in the last three years, revolutionized the world more than any other single person in the entire universe. He did it without money, position, or power, in the sense that we normally view these.

He walked through the country; he talked to the poor, and loved them; he told stories about his Father and his kingdom; he healed the sick and exorcised evil spirits; he played with children;

he drank wine and ate with sinners; he spoke of loving our enemies; he came into town riding on a donkey; he washed the feet
of his disciples; he was beaten and murdered, and he rose from
the dead.

How is it that Jesus had such a profound influence upon his
own, and upon the entire world? Where did he get his power?
From the Father . . . from the Father . . . from the Father . . . from
the Father . . . In the Gospel of John, Jesus mentions his Father
one hundred and thirteen times. If you remember nothing else,
remember that Jesus' primary and constant source was the Father.

You may say: "Well, sure, if I had the same access to the Father as Jesus did, my life would be significant and powerful too."
But we *do* have the same access to the Father. How? Through Jesus. Jesus said:

> I am the way and the truth and the life.
> No one comes to the Father except through me.
> If you really knew me, you would know my Father as well.
> From now on, you do know him and have seen him. . . .
>
> Anyone who has seen me has seen the Father. . . .
> The words I say to you are not just my own.
> Rather, it is the Father, living in me, who is doing his work. . . .
> I tell you the truth,
> anyone who has faith in me
> will do what I have been doing.
> He will do even greater things than these (Jn 14:6–7, 9–10, 12).

Jesus came to this world to teach us how to live and how to
love, and to restore the broken covenant with the Father, in order
that we might share his life and love with the Father forever. In
his humanity he restored it through his faithful obedience (like
Abraham). In his divinity he restored it once and for all through
his resurrection. Even though we, as human beings, may sin and
falter in our relationship (or covenant) with the Father, through
Christ as our mediator, whose story did not end in death but life,
our relationship can be continually restored. All we need to do is
to accept the Father's gift and acknowledge Christ as his Son and
our own personal Restorer, Redeemer, or Savior.

It is helpful here to review the words redeemer and savior in the Old and New Testaments. The word redeemer comes from the Hebrew *gâ al* and it means to be next of kin (and as such to buy back a relative's property, as was the custom then) and/or to perform the part of the next of kin. The word savior in the Old Testament Hebrew is *yâ sha'* and it means to be open, wide or free, i.e., to be safe, to cause to be free, or to rescue. In the New Testament savior means a deliverer, and it comes from the Greek *sōzo* which means to save, to protect, to heal, or to make whole.[4] All the Father wants is our healing and wholeness, and Christ is the most creative and perfect means to achieve that.

In any covenant at least two parties have made a conscious commitment to the relationship. We do not buy a car, a home, or get married without signing an agreement to make payments to the seller or to fulfill our part in the relationship.

Being a Christian means also to make a conscious choice about a relationship (or covenant). But, unlike a human business agreement, there is no hefty penalty or finance charge if we should falter on our part. Instead, there is forgiveness readily available, because the Father's love for us is unconditional, and not based upon our individual performance. All that is required is a genuine desire to respond to the Father's love initiative, through Christ. When we accept the Son we accept the Father, and we also have the complete assurance that no mistake on our part will ever threaten the relationship that has been established.

Sound simple? It is. Many people think that to be a Christian we have to change our ways and live according to a lot of do's and don'ts. Wrong! Becoming a Christian has nothing to do with what we do or do not do. If it were primarily a matter of our performance we would not need Christ; it would be something we earned for good behavior. Becoming a Christian has to do with choosing to respond to the Father's love-initiative by entering into a personal relationship with his Son. It is through our new relationship with Christ that our behavior is gradually transformed.

Let me put it this way: If you had a son or daughter, who had a fifth grade education, would you punish him/her severely because he/she was not performing at a Ph.D. level? Of course not.

Neither does God expect you to be where you are not. The Father created you; he knows you; he expects nothing more than for you to be "you." As you open your life to him, through Christ, you will then (to the extent that you are receptive, and will allow him to work in you) grow more and more loving (in his image and likeness). How does he do that? Slowly, one day at a time—becoming whole (saved), which is what the Father wishes for us is a lifelong journey. Making a conscious commitment to Christ is the beginning of that process.

How do the Scriptures fit in? Well, no relationship can be deepened unless we have opportunities for getting to know the other person better. The Scriptures are the best source of information about the Father and what kind of a God he is, about his Son and his teachings and about the life of the Holy Spirit within us. There are many ways to approach the reading of the Scriptures, and discussion on such is not really feasible here. But I urge you to make this an important priority in your life if you want to grow in the Christian life and in your relationship with God. It is impossible to grow as a Christian without frequent reading of God's Word.

There are ways to know for sure if you have made a genuine and personal commitment to Christ. Generally you will experience the following: (1) a deep sense of being loved; (2) a transformed life, e.g., being more loving and concerned about others; (3) a thirst to know more about the Scriptures and about prayer; (4) a desire to share the experience with another person; (5) a clearer discernment regarding moral decisions in matters pertaining to social justice as well as interpersonal relationships. All of these are a function of the Holy Spirit (the Spirit of the resurrected Lord) who comes to dwell within us permanently when we commit our lives to Christ. The Holy Spirit urges us to grow in holiness (wholeness), and provides for us special graces and gifts to minister to others within the body of Christ (which is the body of believers) and to bring others to the family of our Creator and Father.

If you do not think that you have made a conscious commitment to Christ you can do it right now. It is a very simple matter: (1) ask the Father to forgive you for all the times when you have failed to love as Jesus taught, and (2) tell him that you acknowledge Jesus as his Son, and that you commit yourself to him, and wish for him to be the Lord of your life. Amen! Do not worry about how this will be carried out. You will receive the grace (gift) to do that. God will never ask you to do something without granting you what you need to accomplish it. Remember Paul's words—that his power is made perfect in your weakness (see 2 Cor 12:9).

Exercise:

(1) Close your eyes and sit comfortably as before, breathing slowly, focusing on relaxing your entire body.

(2) Once you have allowed yourself to relax and to achieve a comfortable rhythm of breathing, allow your mind and heart to focus upon the nature of your present relationship with the Father or Christ. Is there such a relationship? What is the nature of it? How do you feel about it? When and how was it established? In what circumstances. How has it grown? What does it mean to you today?

(3) If there is not such a relationship per se, how do you feel about it? Do you wish you would have such a context for your faith and your life? Where are the empty spaces about your life's meaning and purpose that you would like to see filled? What holds you back from establishing such a covenant with the Father and his Son?

(4) Now open your eyes and write about where you are in this relationship, as best you can. Describe the nature of it and the particular issues that come to your mind about it as fully as possible. What does it mean to you for Christ to be the Father's Son, the Son of the Creator? For him to be the Restorer of the covenant with the Father in your life?

(5) If you like, write a dialogue or a conversation between you and the Father, or Christ, about your re-

lationship with him, or the lack of it, and/or about any concerns you have about it, or the effect it has on your life. Let yourself write freely, without censuring your thoughts or feelings.

(6) Read what you have written to yourself, allowing yourself to focus upon the feelings and impressions that come to you about what you have written. Write down anything that came to mind in words, pictures or impressions.

(7) Share your experience with another person, if you wish to do so.

Closing Meditation:

Grow in the grace and knowledge of our Lord and Savior Jesus Christ

(2 Peter 3:18).

Then, just as you received Christ Jesus as Lord, continue to live in him, rooted and built up in him, strengthened in the faith as you were taught, and overflowing with thankfulness. See to it that no one takes you captive through hollow and deceptive philosophy which depends on human tradition and the basic principles of this world rather than on Christ

(Col 2:6–8).

Jesus said:
Remain in Me and I will remain in you.
No branch can bear fruit by itself;
it must remain in the vine.
Neither can you bear fruit
unless you remain in Me.
If you remain in Me
and My words remain in you,
ask whatever you wish
and it will be given you.

This is My Father's glory
that you bear much fruit

(Jn 15:4. 7–8).

For Further Reading:

*"The Gospel of John," *The Bible*
The Dark Interval, John Crossan
Creation Continues, Fritz Kunkel
*Changed into His Likeness, Watchman Nee
More Than a Carpenter, Josh McDowell
*The Kingdom Within, John Sanford
*The Man Who Wrestled With God, John Sanford
A Doctor's Casebook in the Light of the Bible, Paul
    Tournier

THIRD DIMENSION:
"PRAYER AND PRESENCE"

Scriptures:

When you pray, do not be like the hypocrites, for they
love to pray standing in the synagogues and on the street
corners to be seen by men. . . . Go into your room, close
the door and pray to your Father, who is unseen. Then
your Father, who sees what is done in secret, will reward
you. And when you pray, do not keep babbling like pa-
gans, for they think they will be heard because of their
many words. Do not be like them, for your Father
knows what you need before you ask him

(Mt 6:5–8).

Very early in the morning, while it was still dark, Jesus
got up, left the house and went off to a solitary place
where he prayed

(Mk 1:35).

Perspective:

There is no such thing as a relationship without communication. Without communication, a relationship will stagnate and die. Prayer is the way we communicate with God. In human communication there are varieties of expressions, as well as degrees of closeness and intimacy. The same is true of prayer.

The following are four basic forms that prayer can take: (1) In *verbal prayer* we use words primarily, for example, in prayers of petition or in prayers accompanying worship. (2) In *reflective meditation* prayer is expressed primarily through thoughts and images—for example, we may have special insights or flashes of spiritual illumination on a particular passage of Scripture; we may become aware of a new understanding of a passage we have read many times before; we may see it in an entirely different light. (3) In *contemplative meditation* or prayer of the heart, words and symbols still play a part, but they gradually give way to a quiet or stillness within us; sometimes this is also called prayer of simplicity. It enables us to focus our attention more on God and experience a special closeness with him. Finally, (4) when a state of *contemplation* is reached there are no words, thoughts or images. It is a state of deep intimacy with God, where there is only a deep awareness of his loving presence and where we allow ourselves to rest completely in this love.[5]

> For thus says the Lord God, the Holy One of Israel, In returning and rest you shall be saved, in quietness and in trust shall be your strength (Is 30:15).

In order to facilitate a meditative or contemplative prayer experience, and to arrive at that point of quiet and stillness within us, we must begin by, first, ceasing outer physical activity. We often forget that the body, the psyche and the spirit are an organic whole, and that what one is engaged in cannot help but affect the other. Next, we move to silence the inner conversation which goes on continually within and which keeps us concerned with external matters and superficial things. We wait patiently until this subsides, gradually and slowly. Henri Nouwen says that "being useless and silent in the presence of our God belongs to the core of all prayer."[6]

There are several ways to help ourselves to become physically still. One simple way is by focusing on the rhythm of our breathing. Our breathing cycle reflects the state of our body, our psyche and our spirit. In our Western society, we have for so long rejected our body that we have almost forgotten completely the relationship of the body to our encounter with God.[7]

Like all communication, prayer is a two-way street. We communicate with God and we also listen as he speaks to us. Listening is a learned skill which is generally underdeveloped in most of us. Once we experience a degree of physical and emotional stillness, we facilitate listening by the focusing of our attention.

We can help ourselves to pray and to focus upon the Father and his presence in several ways. One way is to focus our attention on an object of creation, such as a flower, or a mountain, or a field, allowing the uniqueness and beauty of the thing to manifest itself to us and thus to speak to us about the love (God) which brought it into being. A second way is to focus on a symbol, such as a cross, and let its meaning be unfolded before us and speak to us about God and our relationship with him. Yet, a third way might be to choose a short verse of Scripture, such as "God is love," or some words of Jesus like "I am the vine and you are the branches" or "I and the Father are one," etc., and repeat the verse slowly, over and over again, letting its meaning develop for us as it will. The same can be achieved with a short personal prayer of our own, such as "Lord Jesus, come into my life" or "Lord Jesus, have mercy on me," or simply with one word, such as "Father" or "Jesus," and repeating it as above, softly, or quietly in our own hearts.

This approach to prayer is taking an open and receptive posture toward the Lord in order that we may listen to and experience his love more completely and be more aware of the ways he may choose to reveal himself to us.

Exercise:

(1)   Choose a Scripture verse that appeals to you, or identify a short phrase, or even a word, which is a meaningful expression of your relationship with God at this time of your life.

(2)   Close your eyes and focus upon the rhythm of your breathing. Let your body and your mind quiet down slowly and gradually.

(3)   Be aware of God's presence within you; let his light and his love fill you up. When you are ready, say the words slowly, over and over again. Let the words adjust themselves to the rhythm of your breathing, so that you can say them comfortably.

(4)   Focus on God's presence; see him there with you, and let the words fade slowly, as they will. Simply be in the silence, as it feels natural for you to do so.

(5)   Allow the Father (or Christ) to love you; rest in him just being there. Listen to him, love him, be with him as you will.

(6)   If and when you are ready, write about your experience, merely describing it as it was. Do not interpret or judge it; only describe it briefly for yourself.

(7)   Write about how you felt about the experience. What was pleasant about it? What was surprising about it? What was difficult about it? Were there any images that came to mind?

(8)   Share it with another, if you desire to do so.

Closing Meditation:

Father. . .
all I have is yours,
and all you have is mine.
And glory has come to me through them.
I will remain in the world no longer,

but they are still in the world,
and I am coming to you.
Holy Father,
protect them by the power of your name ...
so that they may be one as we are one....

My prayer is not for them alone.
I pray also for those
who will believe in me through their message,
that all of them may be one, Father,
just as you are in me,
and I am in you.
May they also be in us
so that the world may believe
that you have sent me ...
that they may be one as we are one,
I in them and you in me.
May they be brought to complete unity
to let the world know that you sent me
and have loved them even as you have loved me
(Jn 17:10–11. 20–21. 23).

For Further Reading:

*The Psalms," *The Bible*
The Way of a Pilgrim, anon, translated by French
The Cloud of Unknowing, anon., translated by Progoff
Doorway to Meditation, Avery Brooke
Our Prayer, Louis Evely
When the Well Runs Dry, Thomas Green, S.J.
The Journey Inwards, F. Happold
The Other Side of Silence, Morton Kelsey
The Practice of the Presence of God, Brother Lawrence
Prayer of the Heart, George Maloney
Contemplative Prayer, Thomas Merton

At this juncture, a Foundations session may be offered, as an option, to participants who wish to grow more deeply in contemplative prayer, corresponding to Chapter 4 of this work, "Classical Approaches to the Spiritual Life."

FOURTH DIMENSION:
"MATURE LOVE AND RELATIONSHIPS"

Scriptures:

I tell you who hear me: love your enemies, do good to those who hate you, bless those who curse you, pray for those who mistreat you. If someone strikes you on one cheek, turn to him the other also. If someone takes your cloak, do not stop him from taking your tunic. Give to everyone who asks you, and if anyone takes what belongs to you, do not demand it back. Do to others as you would have them do to you

(Lk 6:27–31).

Clothe yourselves with compassion, kindness, humility, gentleness, and patience. Bear with each other and forgive whatever grievances you may have against one another. Forgive as the Lord forgave you. And over all these virtues put on love, which binds them all together in perfect unity

(Col 3:12–14).

There is no fear in love.
But perfect love drives out fear,
because fear has to do with punishment.
The man who fears is not made perfect in love.
We love because he first loved us.
If anyone says "I love God"
yet hates his brother,
he is a liar.

For anyone who does not love his brother,
whom he has seen,
cannot love God, whom he has not seen

(1 Jn 4:18–20).

Perspective:

The ultimate test of what we believe is how we love. Prayer is not prayer unless it comes to fruition in love. Praying and loving cannot exist and be whole without each other. If they do, one or the other will be distorted. Jesus' teaching in Luke 6 is a difficult one, because he asks us to love the way the Father does—unconditionally. Loving unconditionally is "for adults only."

As children we seek love and approval, especially from our parents. We size them up to figure out what we have to do to get the love and attention that we need. Some of us work extra hard in school, others of us are "seen but not heard," still others of us do everything opposite to what mom and dad would want us to do to get their attention. We learn a particular technique to take care of our needs for love and security. The problem is that when we leave home, the world is not likely to be what it looked like to us as children. We learned to earn love or to expect love or attention if we performed in a certain way. As grown-ups, some of us are still using the same techniques (e.g., working extra hard, rebelling, being angry or withdrawing) to relate to others, but somehow these no longer work. We are thrust into the world of adulthood, where we have to think and decide for ourselves, and to love freely for the sake of loving, not because we expect something in return.

This is a difficult transition. Often we resist it, and we wish we could just continue on with the old way. It was not all that great, but, like an old shoe, it was comfortable and familiar to us. Like Lot's wife, in the Bible, we keep looking back. It is so difficult to grow up. Whether we do it at twenty-five or sixty-five, it can be so very painful. So, why do it? Why not just stay with our old comfortable way, even though it is limited? Well, we can; that is certainly one option; in fact, many people choose it and never go beyond it. So, why risk going into something new? Because, if we do not, we may be missing the very best part of our lives.

Unconditional love is the greatest positive power that exists in the whole universe. Why? Because it has the capability of transforming us, as well as that which is the object of our love. When Jesus said "Love your enemies, do good to them who hate you, bless those who curse you," he was not setting up a nice little test for his followers. Instead, he was telling us the secret to attain ultimate wholeness and happiness. You might say, "If what we need is love, why bother with God? What do we need him for?" Good question. We need God to move from loving conditionally to learning how to love as he loves, unconditionally. How do we do that? By letting him love us. A person cannot give what he has not got. We need to receive love in order to give love. How do we allow God to love us? By accepting the love-gift of his Son Jesus Christ, and learning from him.

Salvation (i.e., becoming whole) is a process, which definitely started at the time of conversion, but which will take a lifetime to be completed (or perfected). In the meantime, we keep looking to Jesus for direction and strength. We continue to re-examine ourselves in case we have, temporarily, taken him away from the driver's seat of our lives and put ourselves back in that place. Our faith relationship with God is like any other relationship—like marriage, for example; it needs to be nurtured, protected, and affirmed. Christ has given and is willing to give one hundred percent, and all we need to do is be willing to receive his gift and follow his leading. Jesus said:

> Come to me, all you who are weary and burdened, and I will give you rest. Take my yoke upon you and learn from me, for I am gentle and humble in heart, and you will find rest for your souls. For my yoke, is easy and my burden is light (Mt 11:28).

We learn to love others unconditionally by letting God love us. As we do this, a transformation will take place both in us and in those whom we love. We are changed more and more into the likeness of our Creator and Father, who sent us his Son to teach us the way, and his Spirit to dwell in our hearts, until we see him face to face.

Exercise:

(1) Take some time to relax your body and find a comfortable position in which to rest. Close your eyes, be aware of the tension and concerns being released from your body, and receive the peace of Jesus, allowing it to fill you completely.

(2) Review the relationships that you have had in your life, with people who are really important to you and who have truly loved you. Recall them, one by one. Be aware of the transformation and growth which took place in you as a result. Think of those whom you have especially loved. Notice the changes that took place in them because of the way you loved them.

(3) Write down the names of all significant persons, up to the present, that come to your mind. Choose one with whom you may want to dialogue—perhaps someone with whom there is still something unfinished or unresolved in the relationship, or maybe someone with whom you simply feel a desire to communicate further.

(4) Once you have chosen that person, write a paragraph, briefly describing the nature and context of your relationship with this person. Simply state the positive and negative aspects of it, or the general movement of the relationship, up to the present time. When you finish, read it back to yourself, slowly.

(5) Then do a simple outline of the person's life story as best you know it, listing eight to ten stages or steps up to the present time, in order to place yourself within his/her experience.

(6) Close your eyes and be aware of your feelings. Picture yourself with this person at a comfortable place and begin to talk with him/her as you normally would. Write down the conversation simply as it comes to you.

(7)   When you finish the dialogue, read it back to your-
       self, and note the feelings and images that come to
       your mind. Write them down.

(8)   If you like, share the experience with another.

Closing Meditation:

This is how we know what love is:
Jesus Christ laid down his life for us.
And we ought to lay down our lives for our brothers.
If anyone has material possessions
and sees his brother in need
but has no pity on him,
how can the love of God be in him?
Dear children,
let us not love with words or tongue,
but with actions and truth

(1 Jn 3:16–18).

Dear friends,
let us love one another,
for love comes from God.
Everyone who loves has been born of God
and knows God.
Whoever does not love does not know God,
because God is Love.
This is how God showed his love among us.
He sent his one and only Son into the world
that we might live through him.
This is love:
not that we loved God,
but that he loved us and sent his Son
as an atoning sacrifice for our sins.
Dear friends,
since God so loved us,
we also ought to love one another.
No one has ever seen God;
but if we love each other,
God lives in us

and His love is made complete in us.
God is love.
Whoever lives in his love
lives in God,
and God in him

(1 John 4:7–12. 16).

Love is patient, love is kind. It does not envy, it does not boast, it is not proud. It is not rude, it is not self-seeking, it is not easily angered, it keeps no record of wrongs. (Love does not delight in evil but rejoices in the truth. It always protects, always trusts, always hopes, always perseveres. Love never fails

(1 Cor 13:4–8).

For Further Reading:

*"1 John," *The Bible*
I and Thou, Martin Buber
The Art of Loving, Eric Fromm
Big You and Little You, Kristen and Robertiello
Aging, Henri Nouwen
Intimacy, Henri Nouwen
Out of Solitude, Henri Nouwen
Reaching Out, Henri Nouwen
The Secret of Staying in Love, John Powell
Unconditional Love, John Powell

FIFTH DIMENSION:
"RECONCILIATION—CONFESSION AND INNER HEALING"

Scriptures:

Therefore you are to be perfect, as your heavenly Father is perfect (i.e., mature and complete in the likeness of God)

(Mt 5:48).

Who shall separate us from the love of Christ? Shall trouble or hardship or persecution or famine or naked-ness or danger or sword. . . . No, in all these things we are more than conquerors through him who loved us. For I am convinced that neither death nor life, neither angels nor demons, neither the present nor the future, nor any powers, neither height nor depth nor anything else in all creation will be able to separate us from the love of God that is in Christ Jesus our Lord

(Rom 8:35. 37–39).

Perspective:

Some Christians do not like to talk about suffering, sin, or evil; they feel that these are depressing subjects, so they avoid them or deny their existence altogether. Others attribute every-thing negative to the devil; still others talk about evil and suffer-ing with a posture of "Grit your teeth and bear it," assuming a despairing attitude about them. None of these is a healthy and truly Christian perspective.

The resurrection of Christ is the complete assurance that sin, evil, suffering, or death is never the final word in the life of a Christian. Instead, positive transformation and growth is *always* the creative outcome expected. Paul tells us in his Letter to the Romans: "And we know that in all things God works for the good of those who love him" (Rom 8:28).

Christ's desire is that we be mature and complete in the like-ness of God. Many Christians become discouraged or neurotic be-cause they assume that they are expected to achieve this wholeness on their own efforts. If this were so, we would be ren-dering Christ's life, death, and resurrection unnecessary and pe-ripheral to our own salvation.

The power to transform the dark side of our personality, as well as our pain and suffering, is Christ's own love for us and it is readily available for the taking. All we need to do is adopt a recep-tive attitude and be open and willing to receive it. No one can force us to receive a gift that we are unwilling to accept. The same is true of Christ's love for us. He will not intrude upon our private space, or violate our right to make a free choice. He awaits our personal invitation. We can become reconciled and whole as we give him permission to enter into the center of our lives, and especially as we allow him to enter the areas with which we may have particular difficulty.

The root of all sin and woundedness is the absence of love. The major stumbling block for most Christians is not only the idea that God can love them, in spite of their "dark side," but also their own inability to love and accept this part of themselves. This is why inner healing is a resulting factor and a necessary aspect of confession. Reconciliation is bringing together, in love and acceptance, the parts of ourselves which are at odds with each other or with other human beings.

A look at the biblical concept of sin will help here. In the Old Testament sin meant a refusal to know God. Sin is more than anything an attitude of the heart, a conscious and deliberate refusal to love—a conscious choice to turn away from God and, therefore, a breach of fidelity. Another way of saying this is that sin is consciously choosing something other than God's ideal for us (i.e., to miss the ideal, to distort it or to consciously alienate from it, or rebel against it). If we look at the Synoptic Gospels to the words of Jesus regarding sin, we find that his main focus about sin was not in the context of condemnation but in the context of forgiveness. Even Paul, in his letters, tells us that sin enslaves man so that he is unable to do what is right, even when he wishes to do so. Only Jesus, he says, through his Spirit within us, can liberate us from this bondage.

As we look into situations where we have been deeply hurt, or where we have suffered a great deal, it is not sufficient to view these in a rational way, understanding the life circumstances that were involved, and thus choosing to forgive someone, or to accept reality as it was then. It is humanly impossible to forgive without experiencing love, and in many cases the person or situation which hurt us cannot be changed. So how do we deal with that painful experience, or that memory, which directly or indirectly is still affecting our energy level, our functioning, and ultimately our wholeness? Through another person? Yes. In therapy, for example, the therapist's unconditional acceptance can render us the support we need to work through our pain. But therapy is limited to one hour a week for a period of time, and therapists cannot be there forever. We have ourselves forever, and we can teach the "adult" part of us to nurture and take care of the "child" within us. But all of us get tired and lonely, and we do not always have the energy or objectivity to coordinate all our various parts to exercise this process. Whom can we count on, when we are alone and weary, to be always there? We can count on him who said:

> I will be with you always, to the very end of the age
> (Mt 28:20).

> Come to me, all of you who are weary and burdened, and I will give you rest. Take my yoke upon you and learn from me, for I am gentle and humble in heart, and you will find rest for your souls. For my yoke is easy and my burden is light
> (Mt 11:28–30).

Some Christians have a very immature, unhealthy, and unbiblical view of sin. They view sin as terrible things that we do that are against God's law, and for which we therefore deserve severe punishment. It is no wonder that many people want to have nothing to do with Christianity. The root of sin has more to do with refusing to let God's love into our woundedness than with the result of our specific actions. The problem is that we assume that God's love is as simplistic and as conditional as human love. Nothing could be further from the truth. Confessing our sin means acknowledging our woundedness to the Father (or Jesus) as well as the distorted actions which resulted from that, and giving him permission to enter those areas of our lives that he may heal them and fill up our empty spaces with his love and compassion. Confessing our actions, without healing the wounds that initiated them, does not deal with the root of the problem.

In the following exercise you will have an opportunity to focus on your woundedness and allow Christ's love to minister to your needs, so that you may be free to love others in a more mature and whole fashion.

Exercise:

(1) Sit comfortably in a relaxed fashion, as you have done before, focusing on the rhythm of your breathing, in order to become very, very relaxed.

(2) With your eyes closed, allow your mind to be free and open, in order to become aware of the area(s) of your life where you feel you need to grow the most at this time.

(3) Trusting the wisdom of your inner self, allow yourself to picture instances in your life where you have felt most alienated from God and others—for example, times or situations when you may have experienced a great deal of pain or despair, when you felt most ineffective at work or in relationships, or when you were most at odds with yourself. Simply identify these situations or events, allowing them to come to your mind briefly, one by one, without delving into any one in detail.

(4) Open your eyes and list these as they come to you, using a few words or phrases, writing only enough to identify each one. List as many as you can recall.

(5) When you have several of these written down, identify one about which you have strong feelings, one about which you feel there are still some unfinished or unresolved aspects, or one which may still elicit pain, sadness, anger, etc.

(6) Once you have identified it, write about it in your notebook. Describe it as best as you can remember it, noting whatever specific aspects were involved. What was happening in your life at the time? What kind of work and relationships were

you involved in? How did you feel about your life? Do not interpret the situation; simply record whatever comes to your mind about it as best you can.

(7)   Now close your eyes and allow yourself to picture the situation in your mind as you have just described it, seeing yourself there as you were before. Once you can picture it clearly and experience yourself within it, then see Christ, or the Father, entering the situation, approaching you gently and smiling at you, maybe putting his arm around you in a reassuring manner. Then allow yourself to become like a child and share with him your concern and your pain trustingly and in a spontaneous manner, as a child would.

(8)   See Christ, or the Father, listening to you lovingly, ministering to your pain and your woundedness. As he speaks to you, notice how his warmth and his light begin to fill your emptiness and to transform your feelings of hopelessness, despair, or loneliness. See his compassion melt your anger and hate and restore peace and quietness in your heart. Notice how his powerful and loving presence fills and transforms the whole room, as well as everything and everyone else who may be present.

(9)   Hear yourself speak whatever words of forgiveness and compassion need to be spoken to anyone else. Forgive and accept yourself. Receive the same forgiveness and acceptance from anyone from whom you need them. Picture it taking place.

(10)   Allow yourself to experience the love of Christ or the Father. Receive whatever you need from him. Name it, whatever it may be: hope, forgiveness, joy, peace of mind, healing, etc. See yourself relinquishing to him the fear, hatred, anxiety, an-

ger, jealousy, loneliness, grief or despair, one by one. See him receive each with love and melting each into himself.

(11)   See his light and protection encircle you and anyone else who may be present. Allow yourself to receive and enjoy his peace and other positive fruits from this experience, in silence, for a few minutes.

(12)   Open your eyes slowly and write down your feelings as they come to you. Be aware of what may have been surprising, enjoyable, or difficult for you in this experience.

(13)   Share the experience with another person, if you wish to do so.

Closing Meditation:

O God, you know me inside and out,
    through and through
Everything I do,
    every thought that flits through my mind
    every step I take, every place I make
    every word I speak,
You know, even before these things happen.
You know my past; you know my future.
Your circumventing presence covers my every move.
Your knowledge of me sometimes comforts me,
    sometimes frightens me;
    but always it is far beyond my comprehension.
There is no way to escape you, no place to hide.
If I ascend to the heights of joy,
    you are there before me.
If I am plunged into the depths of despair,
    you are there to meet me.
I could fly to the other side of our world
    and find you there to lead the way.

I could walk into the darkest of nights,
    only to find you there to lighten its dismal hours.
You are present at my very conception.
    You guided the molding of my unformed members
    within the body of my mother.
Nothing about me, from beginning to end,
    was hid from your eyes.
How frightfully, fantastically wonderful it all is!
May your all-knowing, everywhere-present Spirit
    continue to search my feelings and thoughts.
Deliver me from that which may hurt or destroy me,
    and guide me along the paths of love and truth.[3]
               (Psalm 139, from *Psalms Now*, p. 211)

For Further Reading:

*"The Book of Job," *The Bible*
The Confessions, St. Augustine
The Screwtape Letters, C.S. Lewis
Habitations of Dragons, Keith Miller
The Wounded Healer, Henri Nouwen
Glorious Victory, Genevieve Parkhurst
Healing and Wholeness, John Sanford
The Experience of Inner Healing, Ruth Carter Staple-
    ton

SIXTH DIMENSION:
"CELEBRATION AND COMMUNITY"

Scriptures:

And the Lord said to Moses, "Say to the people of Israel,
'You shall keep my sabbath, for this is a sign between

me and you throughout your generations, that you may know that I the Lord sanctify you' "

(Ex 31:12).

While they were eating, Jesus took bread, gave thanks and broke it, and gave it to his disciples, saying, "Take and eat; this is my body." Then he took the cup, gave thanks, and offered it to them, saying, "Drink from it, all of you. This is my blood of the covenant, which is poured out for many for the forgiveness of sins"

(Mt 26:26–28).

And they devoted themselves to the apostle's teaching and to the fellowship, to the breaking of bread and to prayer. . . . All the believers were together and had everything in common. Selling their possessions and goods, they gave to anyone as he had need. Every day they continued to meet together in their temple courts. They broke bread in their homes and ate together with glad and sincere hearts, praising God and enjoying the favor of all the people. And the Lord added to their number daily those who were being saved

(Acts 2:42. 44–47).

Perspective:

If the experience of our Christian faith is genuine and significant for us, we will want to share it with others. Can you picture celebrating your birthday, graduation, Christmas, or Thanksgiving all by yourself? Given a choice, very few of us would opt for that. Why? Because there is something powerful and deeply satisfying in sharing a meaningful experience with another person.

Earlier, when we talked about conversion, we stated that there is something very meaningful about affirming what we believe publicly, even if that makes us separate from others in some way. In this section we will focus on affirming what we believe with others who share a similar faith commitment.

The traditional Christian word for worship, "liturgy," means "the work of the people" in Greek. Worship is an act, something that people do. There are five important dynamics that take place in Christian worship: (1) we remember how God has loved us; (2) we offer ourselves to God in response to his loving initiative; (3) we anticipate the return of our Lord Jesus Christ and the ultimate fulfillment of his kingdom; (4) we affirm each other as believers of one body (of Christ, i.e., the church); (5) we share with others the good news (Gospel) of God's love and wholeness (salvation) for them.[8]

Today we find a large variety of styles of worship among Christian denominations. There are certain elements of worship which are common, in one form or another, in most of our churches:

(1) An initial *call to worship* generally opens the service; its purpose is to remind us of the reason for which we gather—to worship God.

(2) It is usually followed by a prayer of *confession* where we acknowledge our sinfulness (our lack of love) in order to prepare ourselves to encounter the Lord.

(3) We encounter him first in his word through the *reading and preaching of the Scriptures*, which serves to nurture us and to help us grow into his likeness.

(4) We affirm what we believe, as a community, in the Creed or the *affirmation of faith*, which summarizes the doctrinal truths or basic teachings of our faith.

(5) Then, in the *offertory*, we offer ourselves to God through prayer, through the sharing of our financial resources, and through the offering of bread and wine (in a Communion service).

(6) The second major way in which we encounter God in worship is in *the Lord's supper*. The bread and wine become for us the means through which Christ offers himself for us as our source of spiritual sustenance and healing.

(7) Sharing the *concerns* of the community, and a *thanksgiving prayer*, may follow Communion.

(8)   The worship experience closes with a *final blessing* where we are encouraged and sent out to continue the work of the kingdom.

The sacraments of baptism and the Lord's supper are among the most powerful means of celebrating our faith and affirming each other as Christians. In baptism we initiate and receive someone into the Christian community. The water of baptism represents the transformation that takes place when an individual makes a conscious faith commitment to trust Christ. Water is a symbol of cleansing and of new life. The new life is due to the Holy Spirit's presence within the new Christian (more will be said about the Holy Spirit in the next section). The role of the Christian community is to stand with this brother or sister, celebrating and affirming him/her in the beginning of this lifelong journey, and offering him/her ongoing support and encouragement.

In the Lord's supper, our resurrected Lord is present in a most powerful and real way. Christ wished to provide a concrete and powerful way for us to be nurtured with his life, with himself. Think about it. Taste is the most intimate of our five senses. We can see or hear things that are far away as well as those which are close to us. When we smell or touch something, it needs to be even closer than that, to be within our reach. But to eat something it must go inside us, and become a part of our being. Jesus wants to be that close. He wants to be within our very beings. He could have chosen another way, but he chose the most intimate of our senses to convey his deep desire to be an integral part of our lives, of ourselves.

Singing hymns of praise, reading the Scriptures, sharing physical and financial resources, special gifts and talents, as well as the joys and concerns of our lives—these are important parts of Christian worship or liturgy. They follow the practices established by our Lord and his disciples in the early Christian community of the first century. Christ's desire is not only that we experience his life individually, in a personal relationship with him, but also that we share the same as a community. He wishes us to have the same powerful bond with him and with each other that he has with his Father (Jn 15:9–13. 17. 20–23).

There is one last aspect of Christian worship which is a beautiful and meaningful tradition observed in many Christian denominations. There are seasons of celebration, during the calendar year, which are assigned special themes, in order to highlight the key events of our faith, our redemption and the life of the church.

The first major season is Advent. It encompasses the four weeks before Christmas. It means waiting and getting ready for the momentous occasion of the birth of Christ. It is followed by Christmastide and Epiphany which celebrate the manifestation of the Son of God in human form—the incarnation of our Lord. The period may last five to ten weeks.

The next major season is Lent which encompasses forty days beginning on Ash Wednesday, during which we prepare for the celebration of the passion, death, and resurrection of our Lord. The original meaning of Lent is the church's "holy spring" in which persons who desired to make their initial Christian commitment were prepared for their baptism. Thomas Merton says that Lent is not a season of punishment so much as one of healing.[9] The season ends with Holy Week which includes a special celebration of the Lord's supper on Holy Thursday, of his death on Good Friday, and of the resurrection on Easter Sunday. The resurrection of Christ is the promise of our ultimate healing and wholeness, despite the human suffering and obstacles which we may encounter in our life journeys. Eastertide is the seven-week period commemorating the latter.

The liturgical seasons end with Pentecost, which celebrates the presence and power of the Holy Spirit within each Christian and within the church overall. The word Pentecost comes from the Greek, and originally it was the feast where the Israelites commemorated the first fruits of the harvest. It is appropriate because for us Pentecost commemorates the coming of the Holy Spirit upon the disciples after Jesus' ascension to heaven and thus the birth of the church as we know it.

Our understanding and experience of worship, as it relates to our Christian faith, is heightened when we are aware of the special significance of each of these liturgical seasons throughout the year. Worship celebrations can become meaningful experiences which truly deepen the faith that we share with others, as well as our relationship with our Lord Jesus Christ.

Exercise:

(1) Take time to relax and be aware of your breathing, and place yourself in a position that is comfortable for you.

(2) Close your eyes and allow your memory to bring to mind moments or experiences when you had a special sense of God's presence, and where you felt a special desire to worship God—maybe in a natural environment, such as the mountains, or the woods, or sailing, or flying, or perhaps at the beach. Think about whatever aspect of God's nature may call you to worship. Or perhaps remember times when you had special experiences with music, or prayer, or sharing some intimate moments with a friend or lover, or when a child was being born, or even special experiences in church.

(3) List several of these briefly in your notebook, simply as they come to you.

(4) Identify one of the most memorable of these times, and picture it as it was. Who was there? What feelings did you have about it? What happened? What about it brought God into mind for you?

(5) When you feel ready, describe it in more detail in your notebook.

(6) What images or feelings were you aware of as you recalled the experience? Allow yourself to write about these spontaneously, without judgment, or evaluation.

(7) If you were to make a spontaneous statement or gesture of praise to the Father, or Jesus, for the gift of that experience, what would it be like? What words would you use, or what gesture would that be? If you would rather convey your experience

through music, dance or another art form, you are welcome to do so.

(8)   If you like, share the experience with another person.

Closing Meditation:

The Lord Jesus, on the night he was betrayed, took bread, and when he had given thanks, he broke it and said, "This is my body, which is for you; do this in remembrance of me." In the same way, after supper, he took the cup, saying, "This cup is the new covenant in my blood; do this, whenever you drink it, in remembrance of me." Thus whenever you eat this bread and drink this cup, you proclaim the Lord's death until he comes. Therefore, whoever eats the bread or drinks the cup of the Lord in an unworthy manner will be guilty of sinning against the body and blood of the Lord. A man ought to examine himself before he eats of the bread and drinks of the cup. For anyone who eats and drinks without recognizing the body of the Lord eats and drinks judgment on himself

(1 Cor 11:23–29).

The body is a unit, though it is made up of many parts; and though all its parts are many, they form one body. So it is with Christ. For we were all baptized by one Spirit into one body—whether Jews or Gentiles, slave or free—and we were all given the one Spirit to drink. . . . Now you are the body of Christ, and each of you is a part of it

(1 Cor. 12:12; 27).

For Further Reading:

*"The Book of Acts," *The Bible*
Whee, We, Wee, All the Way Home, Matthew Fox
Life and Holiness, Thomas Merton

Seasons of Celebration, Thomas Merton
The Genesee Diary, Henri Nouwen
The Idea of the Holy, Rudolph Otto

SEVENTH DIMENSION: "A LIVING MINISTRY—THE FRUIT OF THE HOLY SPIRIT"

Scriptures:

I will ask the Father, and he will give you another Counselor, the Spirit of truth, to be with you forever. The world cannot accept him, because it neither sees him nor knows him. But you know him for he lives with you and will be in you. . . . The Holy Spirit, whom the Father will send in my name, will teach you all things and will remind you of everything I have said to you

(Jn 14:16–17. 26).

There are different kinds of spiritual gifts, but the same Spirit. There are different kinds of service, but the same Lord. There are different kinds of working, but the same God works all of them in all men

(I Cor 12:4–6).

Go and make disciples of all nations, baptizing them in the name of the Father and the Son and the Holy Spirit, and teaching them to obey everything I have commanded you. And surely I will be with you always, to the very end of the age

(Mt 28:19–20).

Perspective:

The seventh dimension of a mature spirituality involves reaching out to minister to others, as a member of the body of

Christ, which is the church. The key to this kind of an effective ministry is a deep understanding of the work of the Holy Spirit within us and among us.

The Holy Spirit equips and enables us to love as Christ loved. There are too many Christians in our churches today fumbling about in various ministries which do more harm than good, because they have gone out to engage in ministry before they are spiritually ready to do so. After Jesus' resurrection, he instructed his disciples not to leave Jerusalem and to wait for the gift that the Father had promised, the Holy Spirit, before they engaged in spreading the message (Acts 1:4–5. 8). The ability to wait for God's time and grace is a mark of the mature Christian.

The Greek word for spirit, used in the New Testament, is *pneuma*; it means breath, which was considered a vital principle of life in the minds of the Hebrews. Even today we speak of someone breathing his/her last breath during the last moments of life. A Christian who is not aware of the life of the Holy Spirit within him/her is as if he/she had no life; he/she is severely handicapped in his/her Christian growth, to say nothing of his/her ministry to others.

In the Scriptures, Paul and Peter tell us that the Holy Spirit is the Spirit of Jesus (Gal 4:6; Phil 1:19; 1 Pet 1:11). Earlier in this work we talked about the fact that the Spirit dwells within a person who has made a conscious commitment of his/her life to Christ (Jn 3:5–7; 1 Cor 3:16; Gal 3:2. 5. 14; Eph 1:13; 2:22; 1 Jn 3:24). In this section, we will focus on what it means to be filled with the Holy Spirit and on the functions of the Holy Spirit in the life and ministry of the mature Christian.

Paul, in his Letter to the Ephesians, tells them to "be filled with the Spirit" (Eph 5:18), and in his Letter to the Romans we learn that this means to have our lives controlled by the Spirit (Rom 8:9). Obviously the Spirit can control our lives only to the degree that we are open to him. Even though we may have made a conscious commitment to surrender our life to Christ, our degree of surrender will vary according to the degree of our spiritual growth and maturity.

All growth, physical, psychological, and spiritual, is gradual. That is how God chose to design it. So, too, our ultimate surrender to the Spirit will occur in a gradual fashion. The more we learn about the person and the work of the Holy Spirit, the more we can choose to cooperate with his grace within us, in order that he can bring us to the fullest state of spiritual maturity possible.

The Spirit performs several key functions in the life of a Christian. (1) He teaches us the truth about God's word in our lives (Jn 14:26; 1 Cor 2:10. 13). (2) He guides and leads us in our actions (Acts 8:29; 10:19–20). (3) He intercedes for us in prayer (Rom 8:26–27). (4) He empowers us (Eph 1:19; 3:16–21) and gives us courage (Acts 4:31. 33; 5:12; Rom 15:17–19). (5) He sanctifies us and makes us holy, i.e., whole (2 Thes 2:13; 1 Pet 1:2). (6) He equips us with special gifts to minister and serve within the body of believers and to further the kingdom of God (Rom 12:6–8; 1 Cor 12–13; Eph 4:11–16). The Scripture passages in parentheses above give examples of each function in the lives of the early disciples. Each of these is also true for us today.

Because of our human tendency to get comfortable and to resist change, from time to time the Spirit within us may choose to break through the comfort in our lives, and, in fact, make us uncomfortable for a period of time, in order that we may continue to grow and be effective ministers of the Gospel, as Christ commanded us to do. All of us can recall a dark and painful period of our lives, where we were having difficulty seeing how a particular life experience could possibly have been part of God's plan for our growth. Later, from "hindsight," it was easier to understand its purpose and meaning, and to see God's hand in the situation.

Our sensitivity to the work of the Spirit within us will determine the degree of our effectiveness in ministry to others. Only by being sensitive to the Holy Spirit can we be enabled and empowered to share Christ with others and thus to love them in a way that they will be transformed, experience the risen Lord, and in turn have a burning desire to share their own experience.

Exercise:

(1) Sit comfortably and relaxed, and close your eyes. Breathe slowly and, as you do, pay attention to the life of the Spirit within you.

(2)   Allow yourself to empty out all the concerns that crowd your mind at this moment. Simply allow yourself to be still in the presence of God.

(3)   Bring to mind slowly the memories of those times in your life when you felt the Spirit was urging you, or moving you in a particular way. Just allow them to present themselves in your consciousness and simply be aware of them, one at a time.

(4)   After a few moments, list each in your notebook briefly, without much elaboration. Go through your list and identify one experience that you wish to explore further right now.

(5)   Sit quietly, with your eyes closed, and picture this situation again in your imagination. What kind of a time was it? What was happening in your life? Who else was there? How did the Spirit get your attention? What happened? How did you feel about it?

(6)   Describe the experience in your journal as best you can remember it. Allow yourself to write freely, without interpreting or censuring your feelings or events.

(7)   After you finish, read to yourself what you have written. What impressions and feelings surfaced in you again as you read it?

(8)   Take a few minutes to be silent again; allow God's Spirit to speak to you in the silence. Listen to him. What are the circumstances of your life right now? What are your hopes and fears about your life today? How do you perceive the Spirit operating in your life? In what direction is he moving you at this time? How is God calling you to express and share his love right now? How do you feel about it?

(9)   How has God gifted you, and what resources has he given you to deal with the circumstances of your life? What, if anything, do you still need? Ask him for it. Picture yourself receiving what

you need. Give him thanks for what you have
and for what you have received here. What com-
mitments are you willing to make to God and to
your brothers and sisters?

(10)   Write freely about your experience and, when
you finish, read to yourself what you have written.

(11)   Share it with another person, if you desire to do
so.

Closing Meditation:

I am the good shepherd;
I know my sheep and my sheep know me,
just as the Father knows me
and I know the Father.
I lay down my life for the sheep.
I have other sheep
that are not of this flock.
I must bring them also.
They too will listen to my voice,
and there shall be one flock and one shepherd

(Jn 10:14–16).

When they had finished eating, Jesus said to Simon Peter, "Simon, son of John, do you truly love me more
than these?" "Yes, Lord." he said. "You know that I
love you." Jesus said, "Feed my lambs." Again Jesus
said, "Simon, son of John, do you truly love me?" He an-
swered, "Yes, Lord. You know that I love you." Jesus
said, "Take care of my sheep." The third time he said to
him, "Simon, son of John, do you love me?" Peter was
hurt because Jesus asked him the third time, "Do you
love me?" He said "Lord, you know all things; you know
that I love you." Jesus said, "Feed my sheep. I tell you
the truth, when you were younger you dressed yourself
and went where you wanted; but when you are old, you

will stretch out your hands, and someone else will dress you and lead you where you do not want to go." Jesus said this to indicate the kind of death by which Peter would glorify God. Then he said to him, "Follow me"
(Jn 21:15–19).

For Further Reading:

*"The Letter to the Ephesians," *The Bible*
The Work of the Holy Spirit, by Special Committee on the Work of the Holy Spirit, 182nd General Assembly, UPC-USA.
Healing and Christianity, Morton Kelsey
The Release of the Spirit, Watchman Nee
Creative Ministry, Henri Nouwen
The Living Reminder, Henri Nouwen
The Christian's Secret of a Happy Life, Hannah Smith
The Era of the Spirit, J. Rodman Williams
The Gift of the Holy Spirit Today, J. Rodman Williams

After this session, if the program is conducted as a group experience, the leader may divide the participants into small working teams and assist them in developing a meaningful worship experience. The group may utilize the eight elements of Christian worship identified in the Celebration section of this work. The overall purpose of this final celebration is to help participants integrate and affirm, even further, what they have learned. For example:

Team # 1 may be asked to write a prayer or find a passage from Scripture which would serve as a call to worship.

Team # 2 could devise an experience which would give everyone participating an opportunity for confessing his/her sinfulness and experiencing the Lord's forgiveness.

Team # 3 may choose the Scripture readings and offer some reflections on the same.

Team # 4 could write up a personal creed or affirmation of faith for the group to say together.

Team # 5 could develop an experience where participants may identify their own gifts and resources and make a special offering of these to the Lord.

Team # 6 could identify shared concerns to pray for, as a group, and devise an opportunity for individuals to express their own.

Team # 7 could devise a way to express thanksgiving and an experience of being "sent out" by the faith community that has emerged in the group itself, followed by a final blessing.

Notes

1. Sidney Simon, *Meeting Yourself Halfway* (Niles: Argus Communications, 1974), p. xv.

2. John McKenzie, *Dictionary of the Bible* (New York: Macmillan, 1965), pp. 818–821.

3. Leslie Brandt and Corita Kent, *Psalms/Now* (St. Louis: Concordia Publishing House, 1973), pp. 211–212.

4. James Strong, *Strong's Exhaustive Concordance of the Bible* (New York: Abingdon Press, 1890), "Hebrew Dictionary," pp. 25, 53; "Greek Dictionary," p. 70.

5. F.C. Happold, *The Journey Inwards* (Atlanta: John Knox Press, 1968), pp. 45–46.

6. Henri Nouwen, *Reaching Out* (New York: Doubleday & Company, 1975), pp. 96–97.

7. Morton Kelsey, *The Other Side of Silence* (New York: Paulist Press, 1976), p. 111.

8. John Coburn, "Contemporary Non-Catholic Spirituality and the Guidance of Souls," *Protestants and Catholics in the Spiritual Life* (Collegeville: Liturgical Press, 1975), pp. 70–71.

9. Thomas Merton, *Seasons of Celebration* (New York: Noonday Printing, 1965), p. 113.

Appendixes

A. THE FEMININE PRINCIPLE:
Elementary or Static

	Positive Expression	Negative Expression
Characteristics:	receptive dark ingoing moist enclosing containing	inert ensnaring fixating holding fast undifferentiated indifferent

Function:	renews organisms
	gestates new drives,
	   images, fantasies
	   and intuitions
	associated with the
	   unconscious
		depriving
		rejecting
		devouring
		castrating
		acting regressively
		associated with
		   collective
		   unconscious

Images:	good mother
	depths
	fruit with seeds
	belly
	womb-shape
	   shellfish
	uterine-shape owl
	casket, coffin
	nest
	cradle
	ship
	mountain (safety
	   of)
		terrible mother
		ensnaring octopus
		ensnaring spider
		suffocating bear

Emotional Responses:	secure protected	inertia depression

	accepted	drifting
	hopeful	paralysis
Behaviors:	trustful	indecisive
	confident	regressive
	secure	fixated
	optimistic	devoured
	protective	addicted
	concerned	

B. THE FEMININE PRINCIPLE:
Transformative or Dynamic

	Positive Expression	Negative Expression
Characteristics:	active transforming liberating merging with another creative	passive destructive possessive enslaving

Function:	urges change
	extends limits
	produces ecstasy
	expresses the non-
	   rational
	leads to emotional
	   involvement
		endangers identity
		leads to darkness
		   and dissolution
		drags down

Images:	birth and rebirth inspiring person child emerging from womb growing fruit seed becoming belly vessel breast	spells of witches devils or demons temptress drunkenness madness
Emotional Responses:	excited vitalized inspired giving	resentment confusion powerlessness out of control losing consciousness dragged down

Behaviors:

opening	retreating
changing	opposing
enjoying	paranoid obsessions
risking	disregarding others
expecting	severing
	relationships

C. THE COVENANT LIFE PROGRAM:
Sharing Expectations

Purpose: This evaluation is designed to assist you to get in touch with where you are spiritually at this time.

Instructions: Please be honest. If you wish, you may write in a code instead of your name. In items 1–5 below, check (✓) in the space provided that which applies to you. In items 6–12, complete the sentences spontaneously, with whatever thoughts come to your mind. There is no wrong answer. Use the back side of the page if you need more space.

1. **NAME (CODE):**

   _____

3. **SEX:** Male   (   )
           Female (   )

4. **MARITAL STATUS:**
   Never married   (   )
   Married   (   )
   Divorced, Widowed
     or Separated   (   )

2. **AGE:** under 30   (   )
           30 - 45   (   )
           45 - 60   (   )
           over 60   (   )

5. **RELIGIOUS AFFILIATION:**
   None   (   )
   Catholic or
     Episcopalian   (   )
   Other Protestant   (   )
   Other (Specify)   (   )

6. I am attending this program because . . .

7. About God, I believe . . .

8. About myself, I believe . . .

9. About my relationship with God, I believe . . .

10. About my relationship with others, I believe . . .

11. About meaning and purpose of my life, I believe . . .

12. What I hope to accomplish through this experience is . . .

D. THE COVENANT LIFE PROGRAM:
Opportunity for Feedback

Purpose: The following items will assist you in reflecting about this experience. Thank you for sharing your learning with us.

1. **NAME (CODE):**

2. List three of the most significant experiences for you during this program:

3. What were the key emotions that accompanied the above experiences?

4. What aspects of the program were most helpful to you? Why?

5. What, if anything, hindered your learning? How?

After you answer each of the following, please estimate the degree of improvement (IR) as a result of this program. Rate them on a 1–4 scale, with 1 = "not improved" and 4 = "much improved." Thank you.

6. What was, for you, the most significant learning about God?

IR = ( )

7. What was, for you, the most significant learning about yourself?

IR = ( )

8. What was the most significant learning about your relationship with God?

IR = ( )

9. What was the most significant learning about your relationship with others?

IR = ( )

10. What was the most significant learning about the meaning and purpose of your life?

IR = ( )

The Lord bless you and keep you and give you his peace
(Num. 6:24–26).

Bibliography

Anon. *The Cloud of Unknowing.* Translated by Ira Progoff. New York: Dell Publishing, 1957.

Anon. *The Way of a Pilgrim.* Translated by R. French. New York: Ballantine Books, 1974.

Augustine, St. *The Confessions.* Translated by Edward Pusey. New York: Collier Books, 1961.

Aumann, Jordan, O.P. *Teresa's Interior Castle.* Tapes 1 & 2. Notre Dame, Ind.: Ave Maria Press, 1978.

Avila, St. Teresa of. *Interior Castle.* Translated by E.A. Peers. New York: Doubleday and Co., 1961.

———. *The Life of Teresa of Jesus.* Translated and edited by E.A. Peers. Garden City, N.Y.: Image Books, 1960.

———. *The Way of Perfection.* Translated and edited by E.A. Peers. New York: Image Books, 1964.

Bechtle, Regina. "C.G. Jung and Religion," *Psyche and Spirit.* Edited by John L. Heaney. New York: Paulist Press, 1973.

Becker, Ernest. *The Denial of Death.* New York: Macmillan, 1973.

Brandt, Leslie and Kent, Corita. *Psalms/Now.* St. Louis: Concordia Publishing House, 1973.

Breton, Valentine M. *Franciscan Spirituality.* Translated by F. Frey, O.F.M. Chicago: Franciscan Herald Press, 1957.

Brooke, Avery. *The Doorway to Meditation.* Noroton, Conn.: Vineyard Books, 1973.

Buber, Martin. *I and Thou.* New York: Chas. Scribner's Sons, 1958.

Campbell, Joseph. *Myths To Live By.* New York: Bantam Books, 1978.

Castaneda, Carlos. *A Separate Reality.* New York: Simon and Schuster, 1971.

Castillejo, Irene Claremont de. *Knowing Woman.* New York: Harper and Row, 1973.

Cooke, Bernard J. *Christian Sacraments and Christian Personality.* San Francisco: Holt, Rinehart and Winston, 1965.

Crossan, John D. *The Dark Interval.* Niles, Ill.: Argus Communications, 1975.

Dieckmann, Ute, Bradway, Katherine, and Hill, Gareth. *Male and Female, Feminine and Masculine.* San Francisco: C.G. Jung Institute, 1973.

Downs, Thomas A. *Journey to Self.* West Mystic, Conn.: Twenty-Third Publications, 1977.

Dunne, John S. *Time and Myth.* New York: Doubleday, 1973.

Edinger, Edward F. *Ego and Archetype.* Baltimore: Penguin Books, 1973.

English, John, S.J. *Spiritual Freedom.* Guelph, Ont.: Loyola House, 1974.

Evely, Louis. *Our Prayer.* Garden City, N.Y.: Image Books, Doubleday and Company, 1974.

Fordham, Frieda. *An Introduction to Jung's Psychology.* Baltimore: Penguin Books, 1963.

Fox, Matthew. *Whee, We, Wee, All the Way Home.* Wilmington, N.C.: Consortium Books, 1976.

Frankl, Viktor E. *Man's Search for Meaning.* New York: Simon and Schuster, 1959.

Fromm, Eric. *The Art of Loving.* New York: Harper and Row, 1956.

Green, Thomas, S.J. *When the Well Runs Dry.* Notre Dame, Ind.: Ave Maria Press, 1979.

Guggenbuhl-Craig, Adolf. *Power in the Helping Professions.* New York: Spring Publications, 1971.

Hall, Calvin S. and Nordby, Vernon J. *A Primer of Jungian Psychology.* New York: Mentor Books, 1973.

Happold, F.C. *The Journey Inwards.* Atlanta: John Knox Press, 1968.

Harding, M.E. *The Way of All Women.* New York: Harper and Row, 1970.

Harkness, Georgia. *Women in Church and Society.* New York: Abingdon Press, 1972.

———. *Mysticism: Its Meaning and Message.* New York: Abingdon Press, 1973.

Hillman, James. *Insearch: Psychology and Religion.* New York: Charles Scribner's Sons, 1967.

The Holy Bible. New International Version. Grand Rapids, Mich.: Zonderuan Bible Publishers, 1978.

Howes, Elizabeth B. *Intersection and Beyond.* San Francisco: Guild for Psychological Studies, 1971.

Howes, Elizabeth and Moon, Sheila. *Man the Choicemaker.* Philadelphia: Westminster Press, 1973.

Isabell, Damien, O.F.M. *The Spiritual Director.* Chicago: Franciscan Herald Press, 1976.

Jacobi, Jolande. *The Way of Individuation.* Translated by R.F. Hull. New York: Harcourt, Brace and World, 1965.

Jaffe, Aniela. *The Myth of Meaning.* Translated by R.F. Hull. New York: Penguin Books, 1975.

James, William. *The Varieties of Religious Experience.* New York: Collier Books, 1961.

Jewett, Paul K. *Man as Male and Female.* Grand Rapids, Mich.: Eerdmans Publishing Co., 1975.

Jung, Carl G. *Aion*, Volume 9ii of *Collected Works.* New York: Princeton University Press, 1954.

———. *Answer to Job.* Princeton, N.J.: Princeton University Press, 1969.

———. *The Development of Personality*, Vol. 17 of *Collected Works.* Translated by R.F. Hull. New York: Princeton University Press, 1954.

———. *Man and His Symbols.* New York: Dell Publishing Company, 1964.

———. *Memories, Dreams, Reflections.* New York: Vintage Books, 1965.

———. *Modern Man in Search of a Soul.* New York: Harcourt, Brace and World, Inc., 1933.

———. *Psyche and Symbol.* Garden City, N.Y.: Doubleday and Company, 1958.

———. *Psychological Types.* Volume 6 of *Collected Works.*

New York: Princeton University Press, 1954.

———. *Psychology and Religion.* New Haven: Yale University Press, 1938.

———. "The Stages of Life," *The Portable Jung.* Edited by Joseph Campbell. New York: Viking Press, 1971.

———. *Two Essays on Analytical Psychology,* Volume 7 of *Collected Works.* New York: Princeton University Press, 1954.

———. *The Undiscovered Self.* Translated by R.F. Hull. Boston: Little, Brown and Company, 1957.

Jung, Emma. *Animus and Anima.* Translated by C.R. Baynes and H. Nagel. New York: Spring Publications, 1957.

Keen, Sam. *To a Dancing God.* New York: Doubleday and Company, 1973.

Keen, Sam and Fox, Anne. *Telling Your Story.* New York: Doubleday and Company, 1973.

Kelsey, Morton. *Adventure Inward.* Minneapolis, Minn.: Augsburg House, 1980.

———. *Discernment.* New York: Paulist Press, 1978.

———. *Encounter with God.* Minneapolis, Minn.: Bethany Fellowship, 1972.

———. *Healing and Christianity.* New York: Harper and Row, 1973.

———. *Myth, History and Faith.* New York: Paulist Press, 1974.

———. *The Other Side of Silence.* New York: Paulist Press, 1976.

Kempis, Thomas A. *The Imitation of Christ.* Garden City, N.Y.: Image Books, 1955.

Kopp, Sheldon B. *If You Meet the Buddah on the Road, Kill Him!* New York: Bantam Books, 1972.

Kristen, G. and Robertiello, R. *Big You and Little You.* New York: Pocket Books, 1977.

Kübler-Ross, Elisabeth. *Death and Dying.* New York: Macmillan, Inc., 1969.

———. *Death, the Final Stage of Growth.* Englewood Cliffs, N.J.: Prentice-Hall, 1975.

Küng, Hans. *On Being a Christian.* Translated by E. Quinn. New York: Pocket Books, 1976.

Kunkel, Fritz. *Creation Continues.* Waco, Texas: Word Books, 1973.

Lawrence, Brother. *The Practice of the Presence of God.* Edited by Donald Demaray. Grand Rapids, Mich.: Baker Book House, 1975.

LeShan, Eda. *The Wonderful Crisis of Middle Age.* New York: David McKay Company, Inc., 1973.

LeShan, Lawrence. *How To Meditate.* New York: Little, Brown and Co., 1974.

Lewis, C.S. *Mere Christianity.* New York: Macmillan Publishing Co., 1952.

——. *The Screwtape Letters.* New York: Macmillan Publishing Co., 1961.

Lindberg, Anne M. *Gifts from the Sea.* New York: Pantheon Books, 1955.

Loyola, St. Ignatius of. *The Spiritual Exercises.* Translated by A. Mottola. New York: Doubleday and Co., 1964.

Maloney, George, S.J. *Prayer of the Heart.* Notre Dame, Ind.: Ave Maria Press, 1981.

Mark, Michael, O.S.B., ed. *Protestants and Catholics on the Spiritual Life.* Collegeville, Minn.: The Liturgical Press, 1965.

Maslow, Abraham H. *Farther Reaches of Human Nature.* New York: Viking Press, 1971.

——. "Religion and Peak Experiences," *Psyche and Spirit.* Edited by John L. Heaney. New York: Paulist Press, 1973.

Meisel, Anthony and del Mastro, M. *The Rule of St. Benedict.* Garden City, N.Y.: Image Books, 1975.

Menninger, Karl. *Whatever Happened to Sin?* New York: Hawthorne Press, 1973.

Merton, Thomas. *Contemplative Prayer.* Garden City, N.Y.: Doubleday and Company, 1968.

——. *Life and Holiness.* New York: Doubleday and Company, 1964.

——. *No Man Is an Island.* Garden City, N.Y.: Image Books, 1967.

——. *New Seeds of Contemplation.* New York: New Directions Publishing Company, 1972.

————. *Seasons of Celebration.* New York: Noonday Printing, 1965.

Miller, Keith. *Habitations of Dragons.* Waco, Texas: Word Books, 1970.

————. *The Taste of New Wine.* New York: Bantam Books, 1965.

McDowell, Josh. *More Than a Carpenter.* Wheaton, Ill.: Tyndale House Publishing., 1977.

McKenzie, John. *Dictionary of the Bible.* New York: Macmillan Publishing Co., 1965.

Nee, Watchman. *Changed into His Likeness.* Fort Washington, Penn.: Christian Literature Crusade, 1967.

————. *The Release of the Spirit.* Cloverdale, Ind.: Sure Foundation, 1965.

Nouwen, Henri. *Aging.* Garden City, N.Y.: Image Books, 1974.

————. *Creative Ministry.* New York: Doubleday and Company, 1971.

————. *The Genesee Diary.* New York: Doubleday and Company, 1976.

————. *Intimacy.* Notre Dame, Ind.: Fides/Claretian Publishers, 1969.

————. *The Living Reminder.* New York: Seabury Press, 1977.

————. *Out of Solitude.* Notre Dame, Ind.: Ave Maria Press, 1974.

————. *Pray To Live.* Notre Dame, Ind.: Fides Publishing Co., Inc., 1972.

————. *Reaching Out.* New York: Doubleday and Company, 1975.

————. *The Wounded Healer.* New York: Doubleday and Company, 1972.

Novak, Michael. *Ascent of the Mountain and Flight of the Dove.* New York: Harper and Row, 1971.

O'Connor, Elizabeth. *Journey Inward, Journey Outward.* New York: Harper and Row, 1968.

————. *Search for Silence.* Waco, Texas: Word Books, 1972.

Ornstein, Robert E. *The Psychology of Consciousness.* New York: Penguin Books, 1972.

Otto, Rudolph. *The Idea of the Holy.* New York: Oxford Press, 1958.

Parkhurst, Genevieve. *Glorious Victory.* St. Paul, Minn.: Macalester Park Pub., 1973.

Pennington, M. Basil. *Daily We Touch Him.* Garden City, N.Y.: Image Books, 1979.

Pirsig, Robert M. *Zen and the Art of Motorcycle Maintenance.* New York: Bantam Book, 1974.

Poshesney, Venard O. *Attaining Spiritual Maturity for Contemplation According to St. John of the Cross.* Locust Valley, N.Y.: Living Flame Press, 1973.

Powell, John. *The Secret of Staying in Love.* Niles, Ill.: Argus Communications, 1974.

———. *Unconditional Love.* Niles, Ill.: Argus Communications, 1978.

Progoff, Ira. *At a Journal Workshop.* New York: Dialogue House, 1975.

———. *Depth Psychology and Modern Man.* New York: McGraw-Hill, 1959.

———. *Jung, Synchronicity and Human Destiny.* New York: Dell Publishing Co., 1973.

———. *The Symbolic and the Real.* New York: McGraw-Hill, 1963

Rahner, Hugo, S.J. *The Spirituality of St. Ignatius of Loyola.* Translated by J. Smith. Chicago: Loyola University Press, 1953.

Rahner, Karl. *Belief Today.* New York: Sheed and Ward, 1967.

———. *Encounter with Silence.* Westminster, Md.: Newman Press, 1960.

Reid, Clyde. *The Return to Faith.* New York: Harper and Row, 1974.

Ruether, Rosemary R. *Mary—The Feminine Face of the Church.* Philadelphia: Westminster Press, 1977.

Sanford, Agnes. *The Healing Gifts of the Spirit.* New York: A.J. Holman Co., 1966.

Sanford, John. *Dreams, God's Forgotten Language.* New York: J.B. Lippincott Co., 1968.

————. *Healing and Wholeness.* New York: Paulist Press, 1971.

————. *The Kingdom Within.* New York: J.B. Lippincott, 1970.

————. *The Man Who Wrestled With God.* King of Prussia, Pa.: Religious Publishing Co., 1974.

Sheehy, Gail. *Passages.* New York: E.P. Dutton and Co., 1976.

Simon, Sidney. *Meeting Yourself Halfway.* Niles, Ill.: Argus Communications, 1974.

Special Committee on the Work of the Holy Spirit. *The Work of the Holy Spirit.* 182nd General Assembly, U.P.C.-U.S.A.

Simons, George. *Keeping a Personal Journal.* New York: Paulist Press, 1973.

Singer, June. *Androgeny.* New York: Doubleday, 1976.

————. *Boundaries of the Soul.* Garden City, N.Y.: Anchor Books, 1972.

Smith, Hannah W. *The Christian's Secret of a Happy Life.* New Jersey: Pyramid Publications, 1976.

Stapleton Ruth C. *The Experience of Inner Healing.* Waco, Texas: Word Books, 1977.

Stendahl, Kristen. *The Bible and the Role of Women.* Philadelphia: Fortress Press, 1966.

Strong, James. *Strong's Exhaustive Concordance of the Bible.* New York: Abingdon Press, 1890.

Tillich, Paul. *Dynamics of Faith.* New York: Harper Colophon Books, 1957.

————. *My Search for Absolutes.* New York: Simon and Schuster, 1967.

Tournier, Paul. *A Doctor's Casebook in the Light of the Bible.* Translated by E. Hudson, New York: Harper and Row, 1960.

————. *The Meaning of Persons.* New York: Harper and Row, 1957.

Ulanov, Ann B. *The Feminine.* Evanston: Northwestern University Press, 1971.

Ulanov, Ann and Ulanov, Barry. *Religion and the Unconscious.* Philadelphia: Westminster Press, 1975.

Underhill, Evelyn. *Practical Mysticism.* New York: E.P. Dutton and Company, 1943.

————. *Mystics of the Church.* Cambridge: James Clarke and Company, 1975.

————. *The Spiritual Life.* New York: Harper and Row, n.d.

Van Kaam, Adrian. *Spirituality and the Gentle Life.* Denville, N.J.: Dimension Books, 1974.

Von Franz, Marie L. *The Feminine in Fairytales.* New York: Spring Publications, 1976.

Von Franz, Marie L. and Hillman, James. *Jung's Typology.* New York: Spring Publications, 1971.

Weil, Simone. *Waiting for God.* New York: Harper and Row, 1951.

Wickes, Frances G. *The Inner World of Choice.* Englewood Cliffs, N.J.: Prentice-Hall, 1963.

Williams, J. Rodman. *The Era of the Spirit.* Plainfield, N.J.: Logos International, 1971.

————. *The Gift of the Holy Spirit Today.* New Jersey: Logos International, 1980.

Wink, Walter. *The Bible in Human Transformation.* Philadelphia: Fortress Press, 1973.

What are the conditions
that support spiritual growth?

Lifestyle which I hope
flows from God's
purposes ... choose
what values I have
in rela to God.

Develop a way of living
that supports ... guides our
journey
New year - new look at where going